Terrible Means

IN THE FINAL DAYS OF THE EMPIRE
AS THE PEOPLE AWOKE,
RED CARNATION, IT WAS YOUR SMILE
THAT TOLD US ALL WAS REBORN

— LOUISE MICHEL

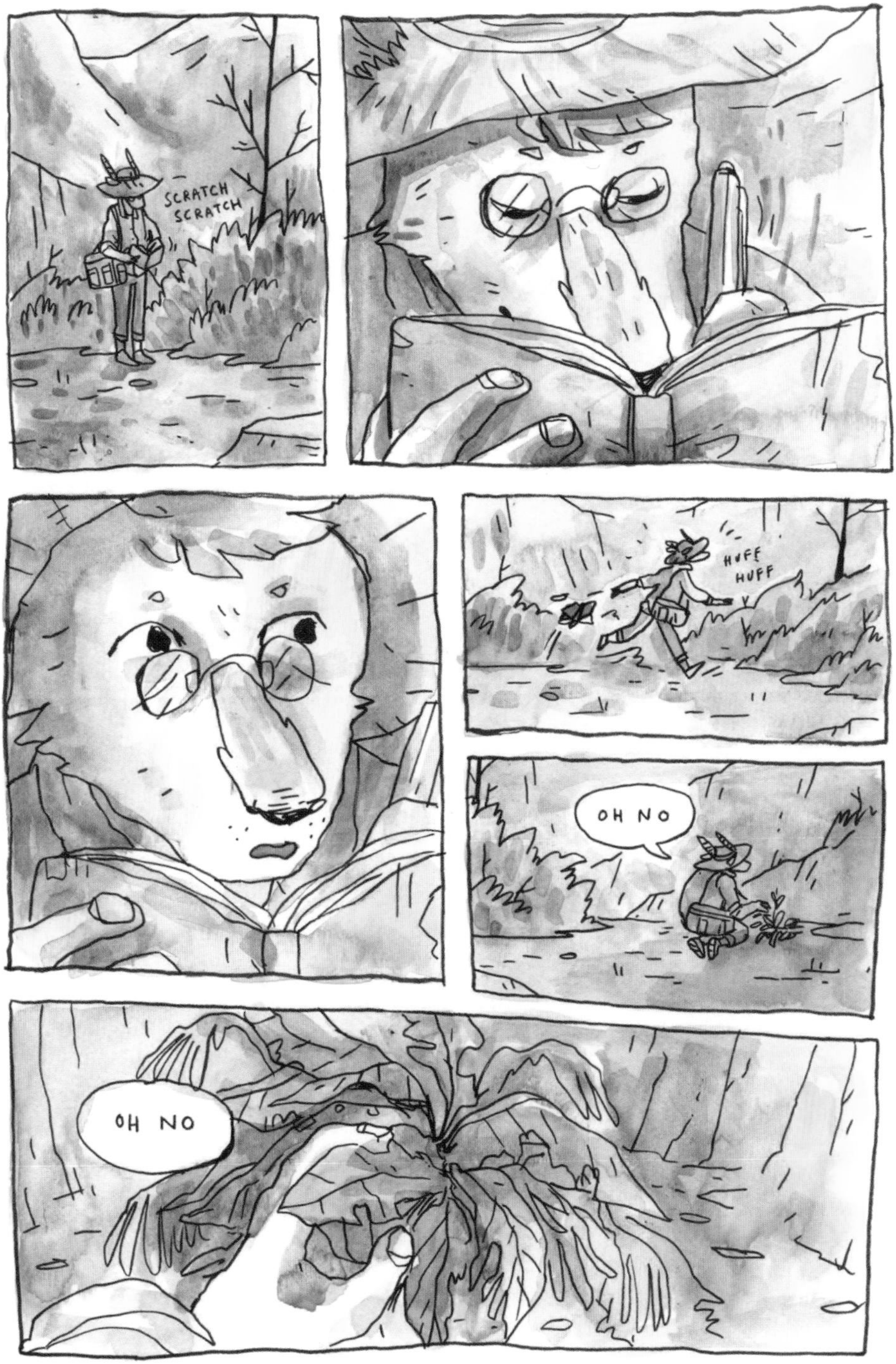
SCRATCH
SCRATCH
HUFF
HUFF
OH NO
OH NO

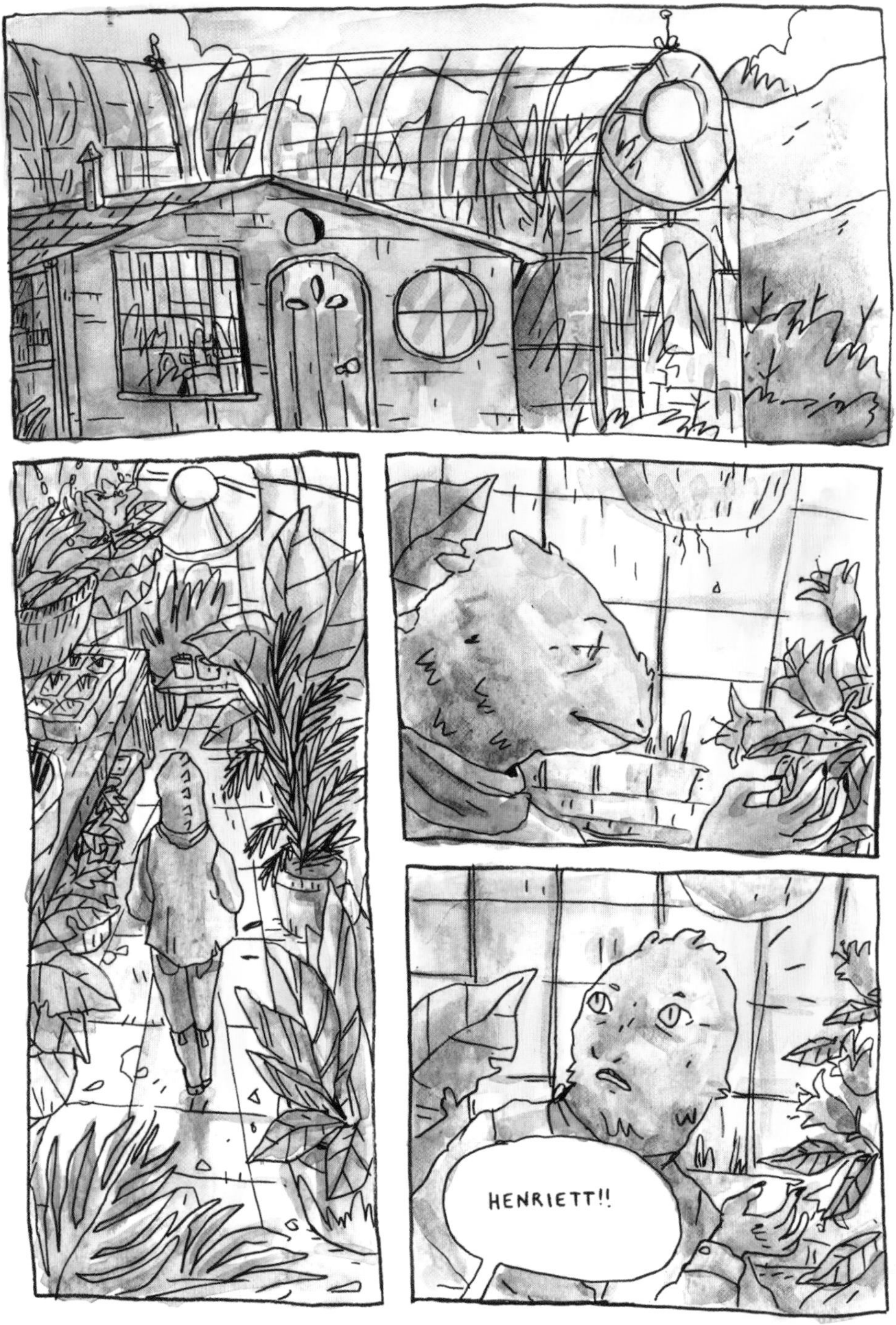
HENRIETT!!

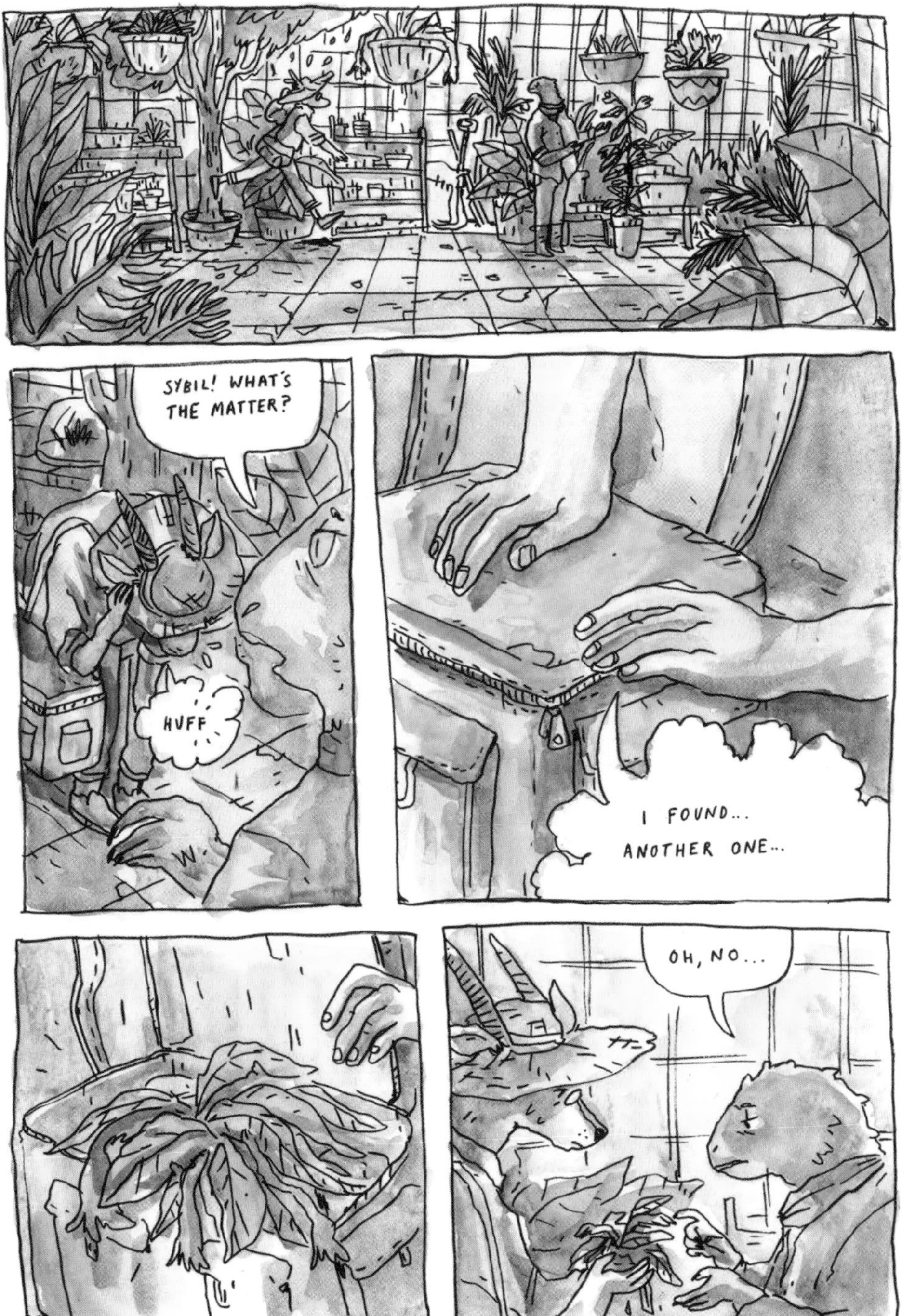
SYBIL! WHAT'S THE MATTER?
HUFF
I FOUND... ANOTHER ONE...
OH, NO...

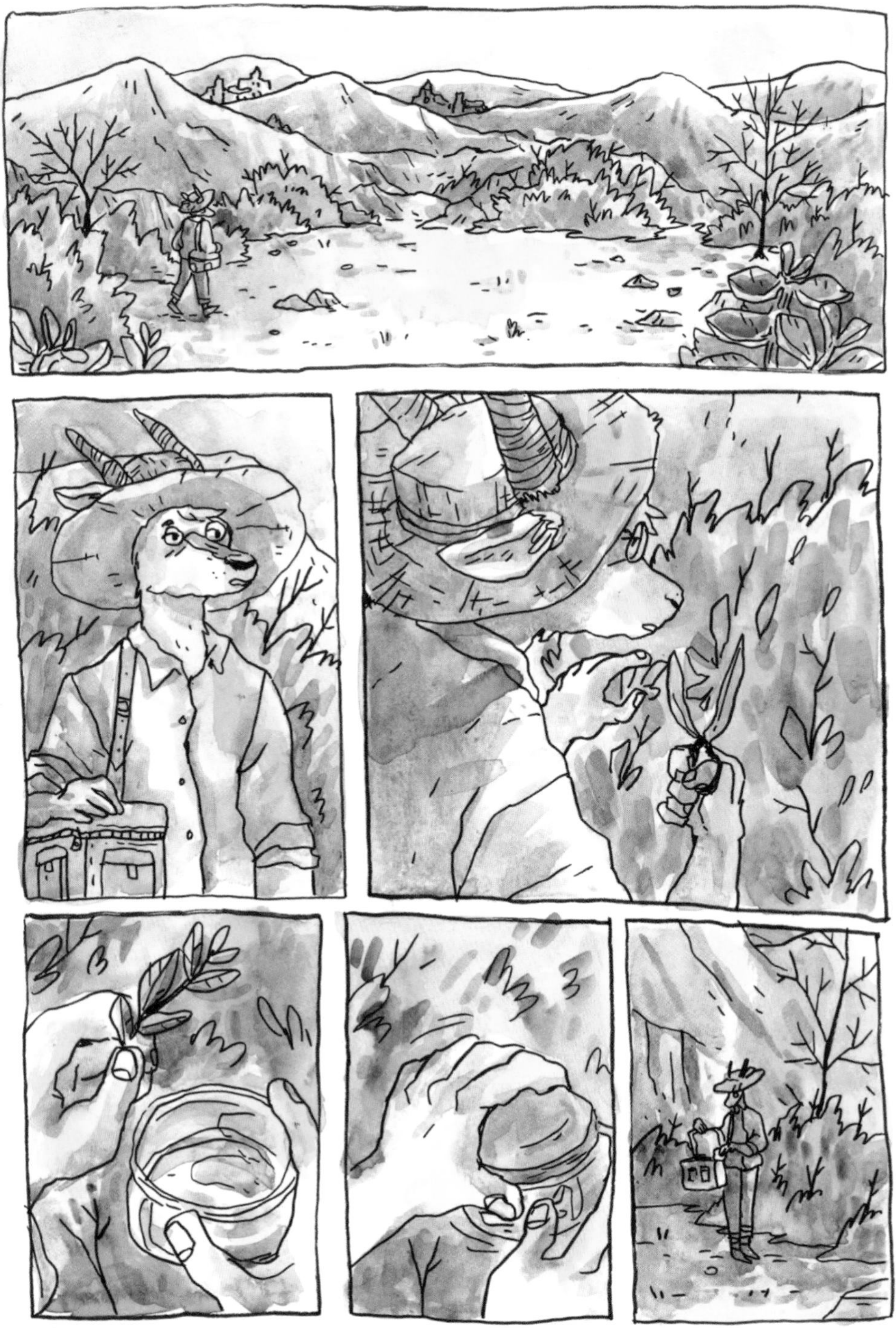

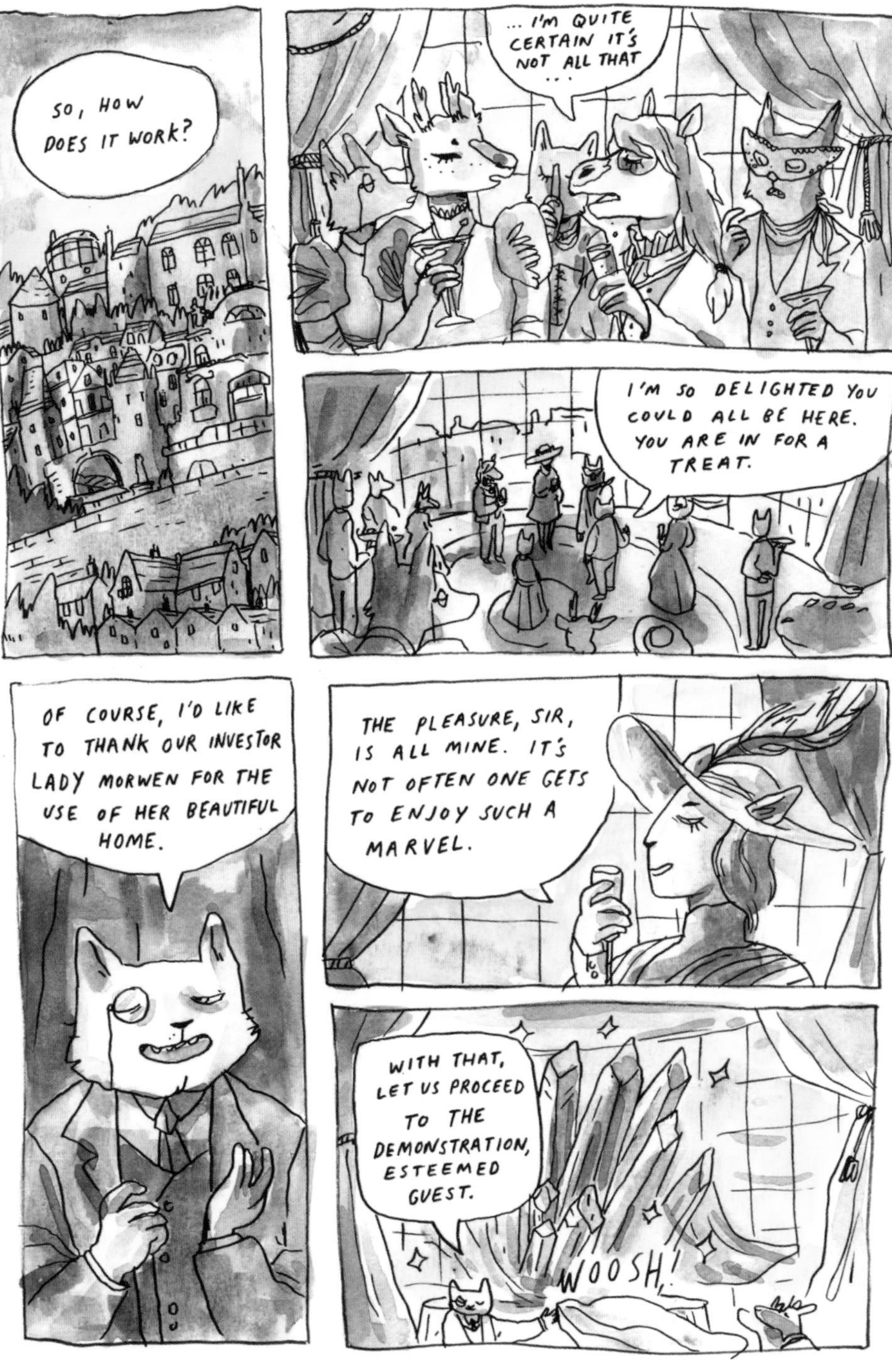
SO, HOW DOES IT WORK?
... I'M QUITE CERTAIN IT'S NOT ALL THAT ...
I'M SO DELIGHTED YOU COULD ALL BE HERE. YOU ARE IN FOR A TREAT.
OF COURSE, I'D LIKE TO THANK OUR INVESTOR LADY MORWEN FOR THE USE OF HER BEAUTIFUL HOME.
THE PLEASURE, SIR, IS ALL MINE. IT'S NOT OFTEN ONE GETS TO ENJOY SUCH A MARVEL.
WITH THAT, LET US PROCEED TO THE DEMONSTRATION, ESTEEMED GUEST.
WOOSH!

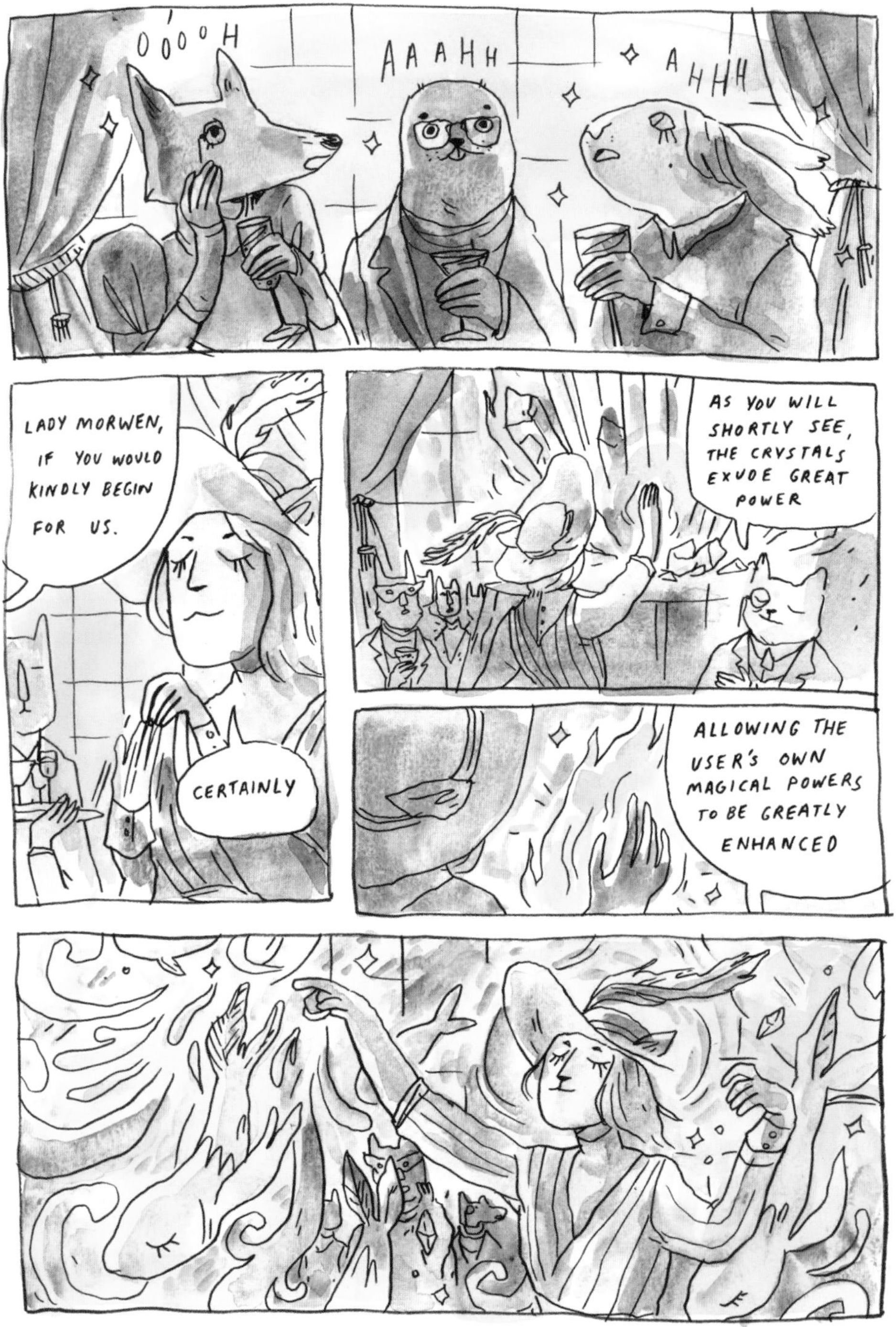
OOOOH
AAAHH
AHHH
LADY MORWEN, IF YOU WOULD KINDLY BEGIN FOR US.
CERTAINLY
AS YOU WILL SHORTLY SEE, THE CRYSTALS EXUDE GREAT POWER
ALLOWING THE USER'S OWN MAGICAL POWERS TO BE GREATLY ENHANCED

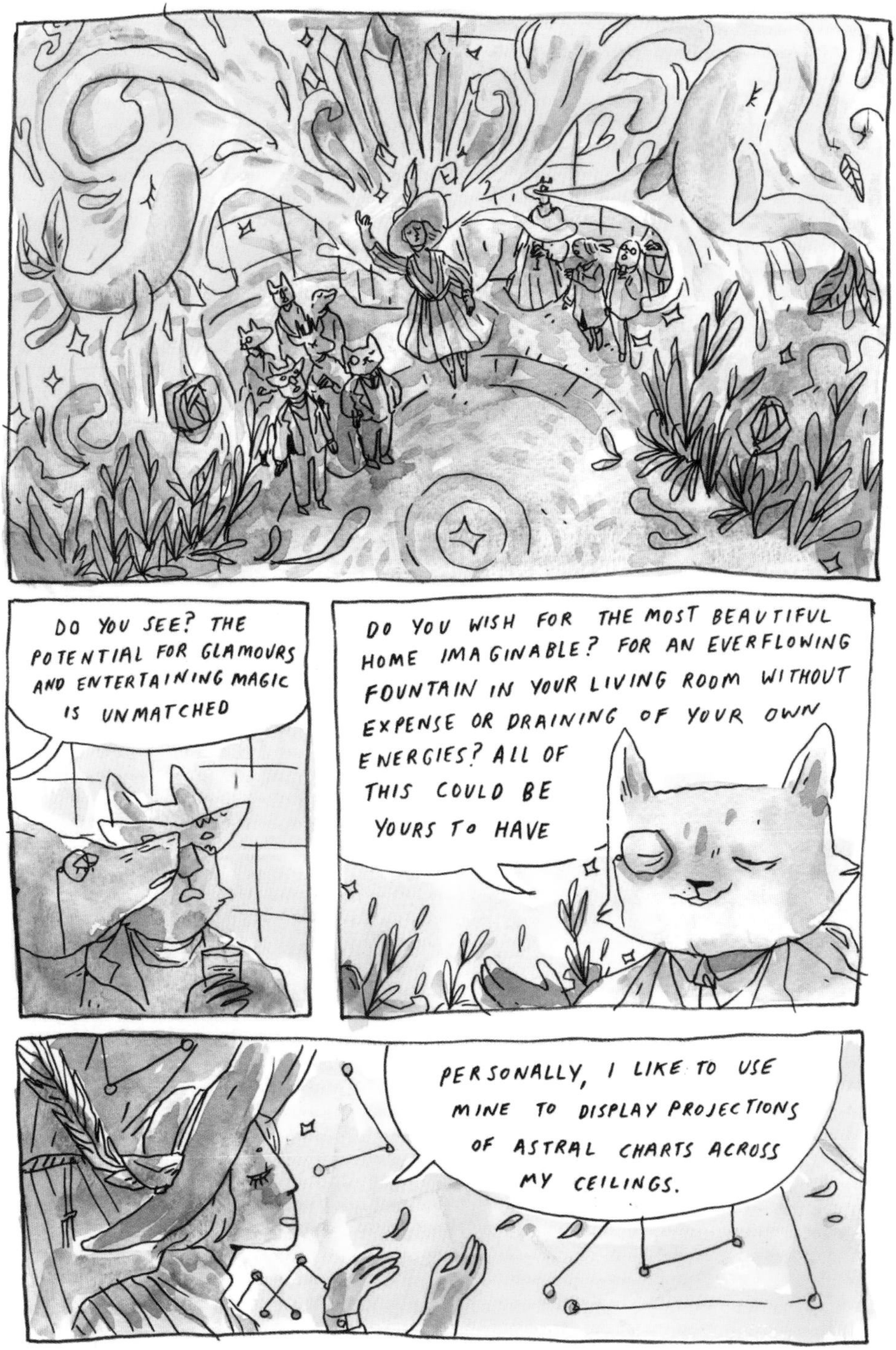
DO YOU SEE? THE POTENTIAL FOR GLAMOURS AND ENTERTAINING MAGIC IS UNMATCHED
DO YOU WISH FOR THE MOST BEAUTIFUL HOME IMAGINABLE? FOR AN EVERFLOWING FOUNTAIN IN YOUR LIVING ROOM WITHOUT EXPENSE OR DRAINING OF YOUR OWN ENERGIES? ALL OF THIS COULD BE YOURS TO HAVE
PERSONALLY, I LIKE TO USE MINE TO DISPLAY PROJECTIONS OF ASTRAL CHARTS ACROSS MY CEILINGS.

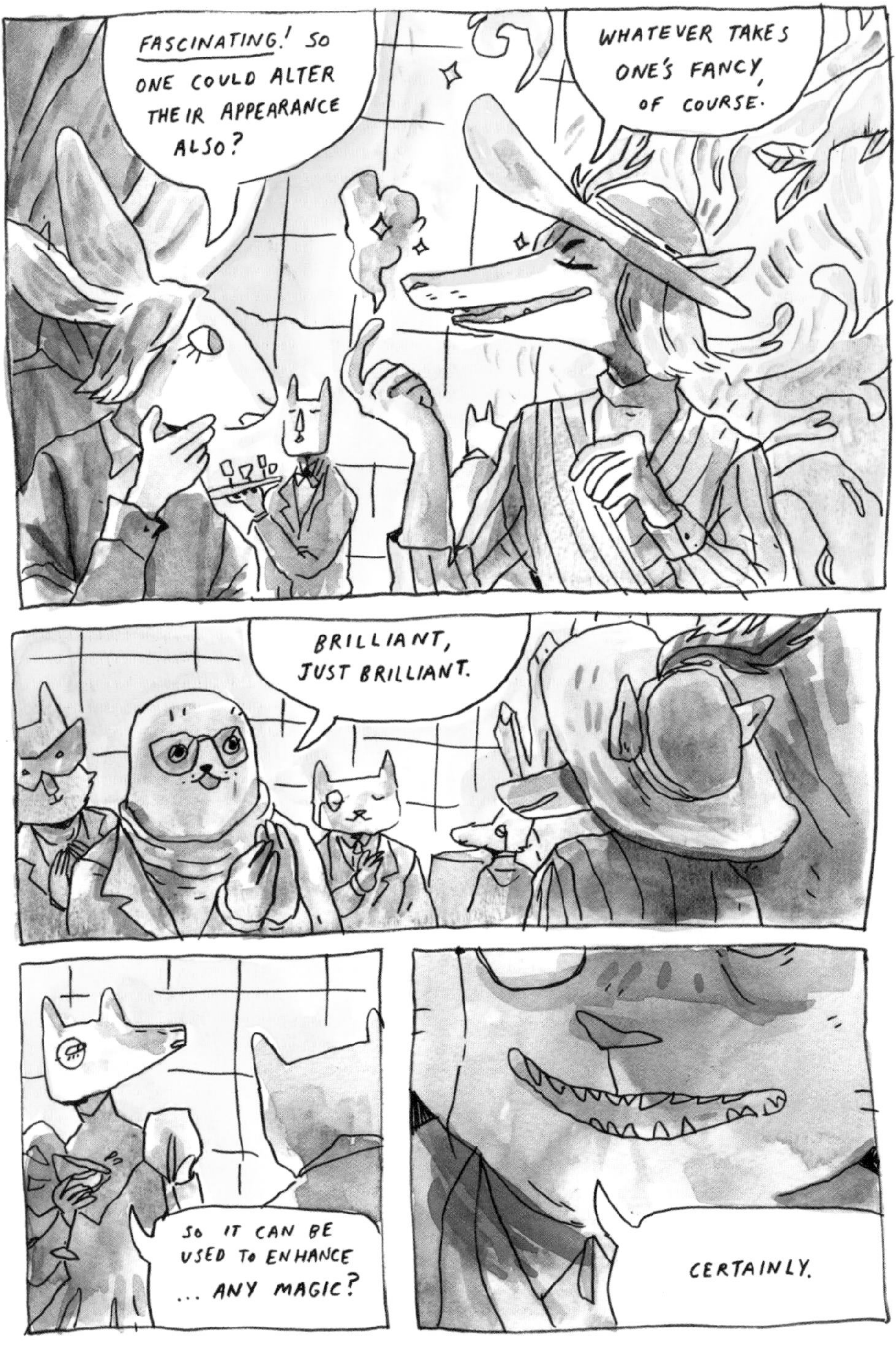
FASCINATING! SO ONE COULD ALTER THEIR APPEARANCE ALSO?
WHATEVER TAKES ONE'S FANCY, OF COURSE.
BRILLIANT, JUST BRILLIANT.
SO IT CAN BE USED TO ENHANCE ... ANY MAGIC?
CERTAINLY.

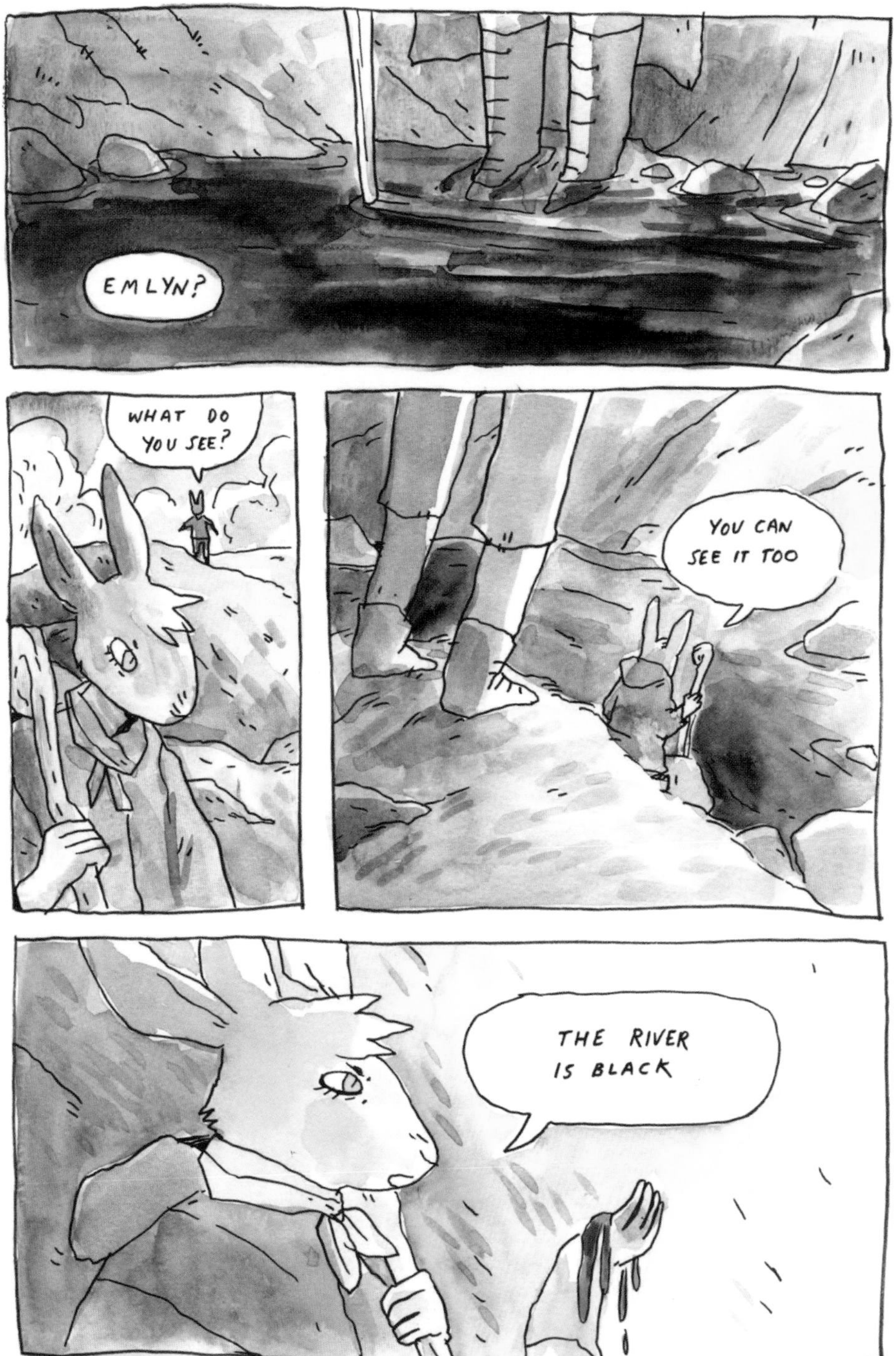
EMLYN?
WHAT DO YOU SEE?
YOU CAN SEE IT TOO
THE RIVER IS BLACK

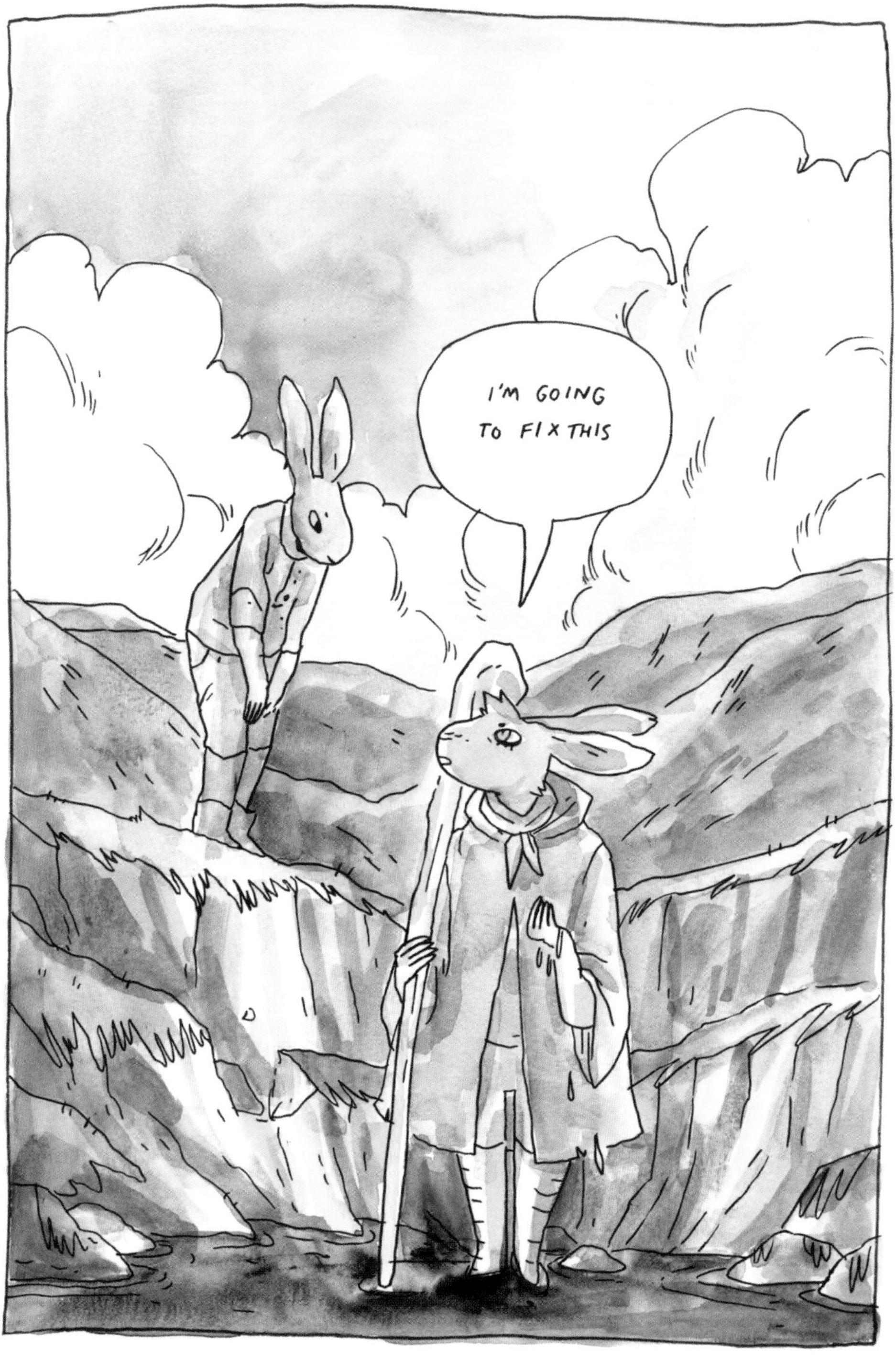
I'M GOING TO FIX THIS

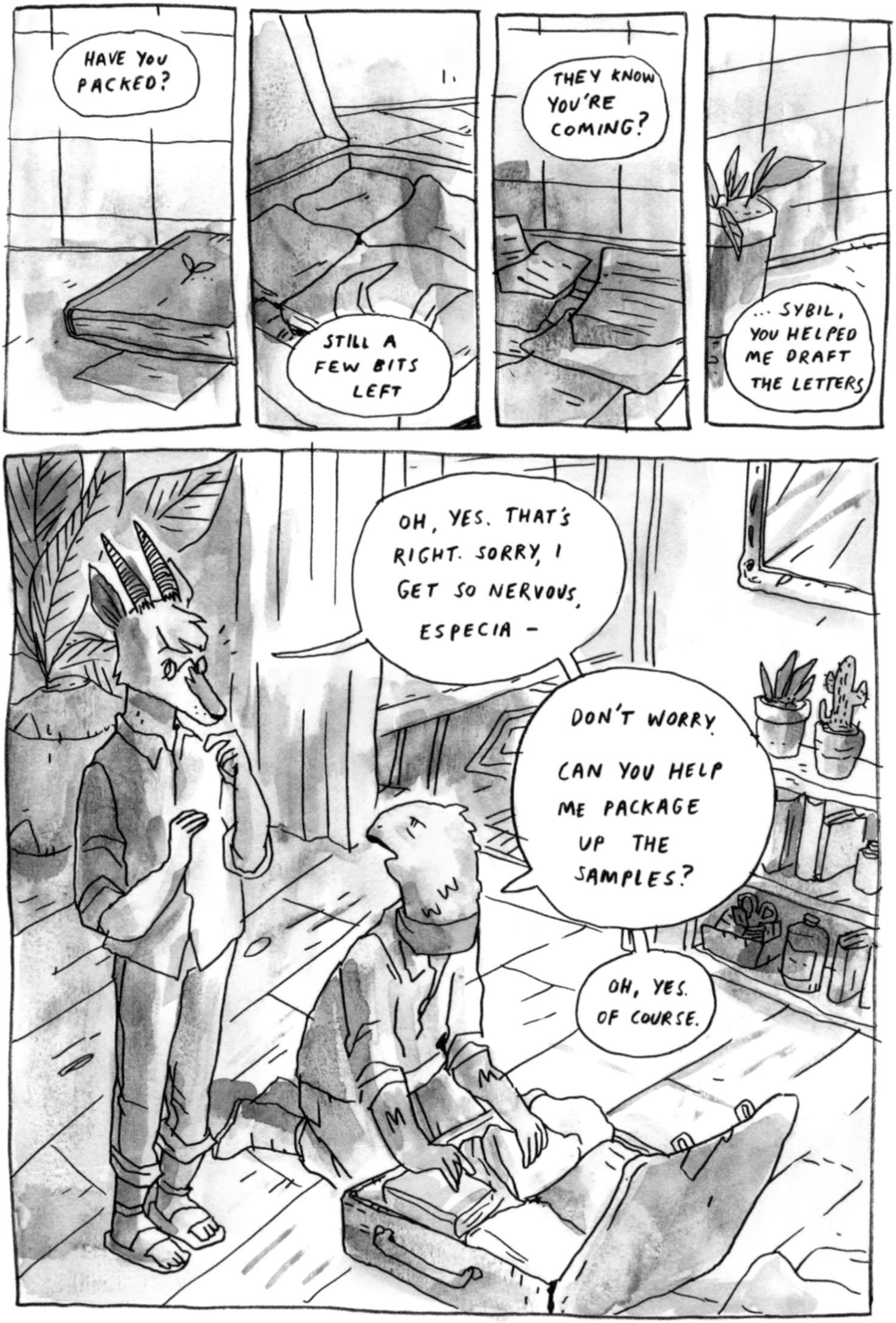
HAVE YOU PACKED?
STILL A FEW BITS LEFT
THEY KNOW YOU'RE COMING?
... SYBIL, YOU HELPED ME DRAFT THE LETTERS
OH, YES. THAT'S RIGHT. SORRY, I GET SO NERVOUS, ESPECIA -
DON'T WORRY.
CAN YOU HELP ME PACKAGE UP THE SAMPLES?
OH, YES. OF COURSE.

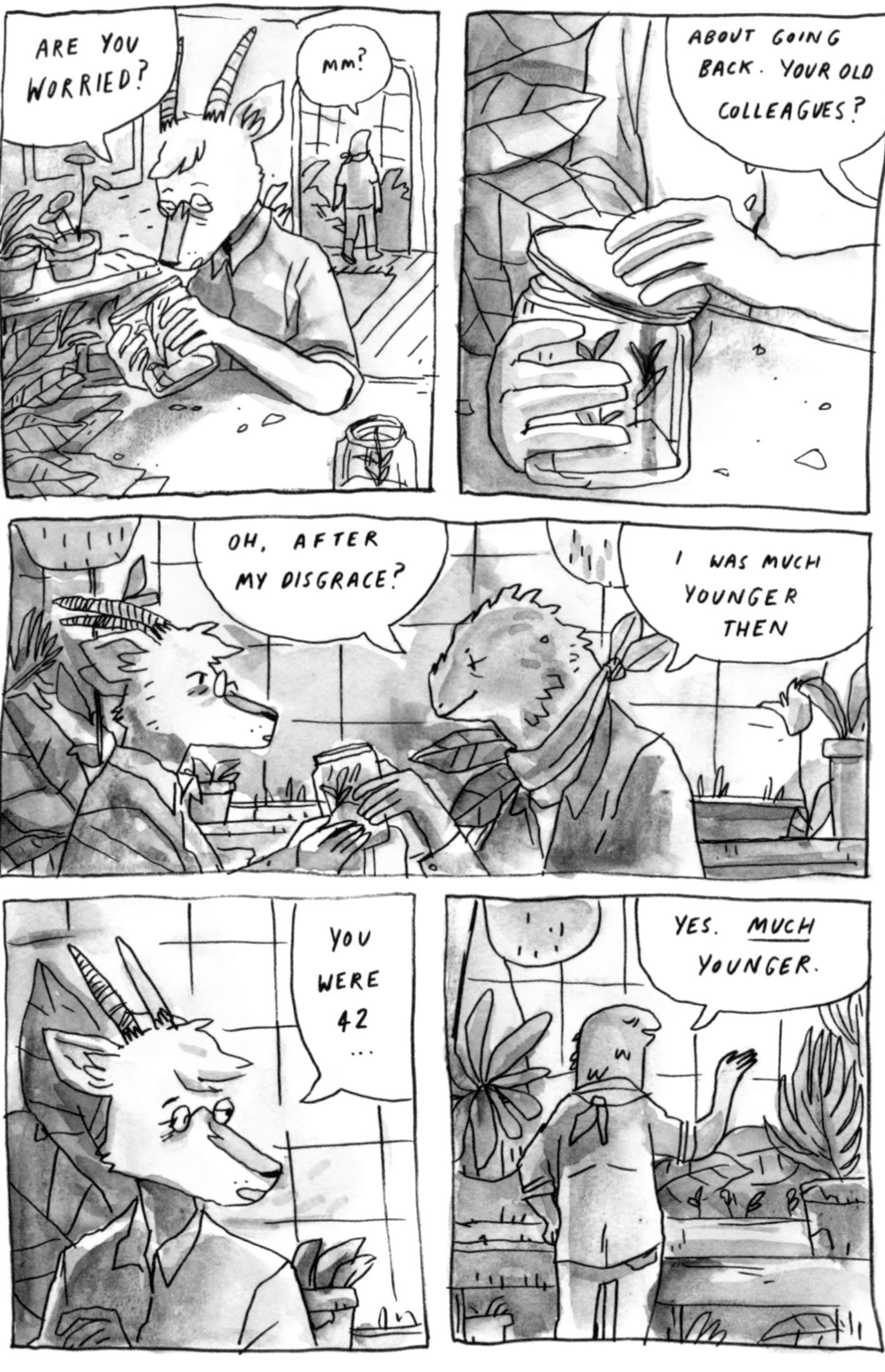
ARE YOU WORRIED?
MM?
ABOUT GOING BACK. YOUR OLD COLLEAGUES?
OH, AFTER MY DISGRACE?
I WAS MUCH YOUNGER THEN
YOU WERE 42 ...
YES. MUCH YOUNGER.

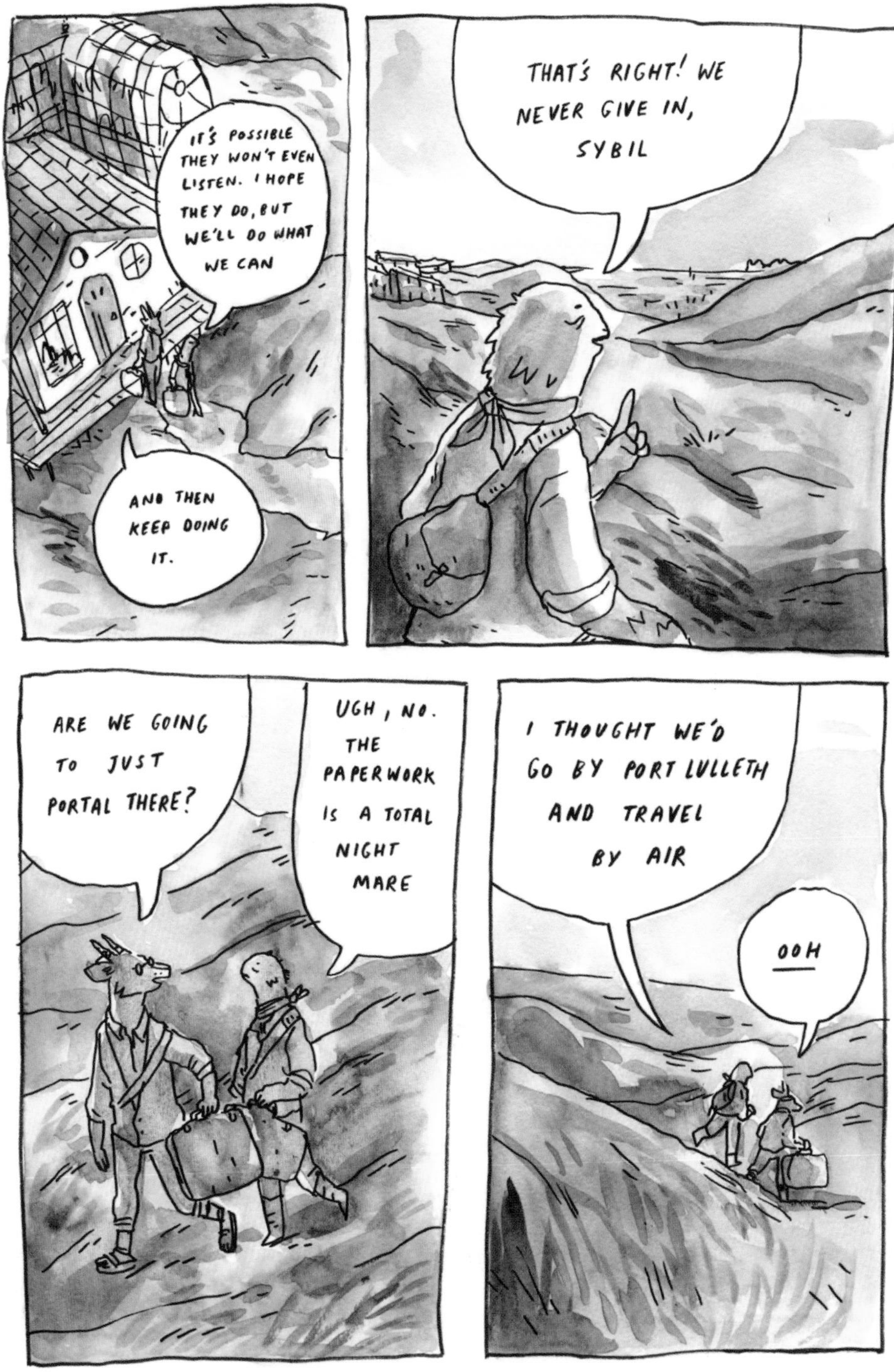
IT'S POSSIBLE THEY WON'T EVEN LISTEN. I HOPE THEY DO, BUT WE'LL DO WHAT WE CAN
AND THEN KEEP DOING IT.
THAT'S RIGHT! WE NEVER GIVE IN, SYBIL
ARE WE GOING TO JUST PORTAL THERE?
UGH, NO. THE PAPERWORK IS A TOTAL NIGHT MARE
I THOUGHT WE'D GO BY PORT LULLETH AND TRAVEL BY AIR
OOH

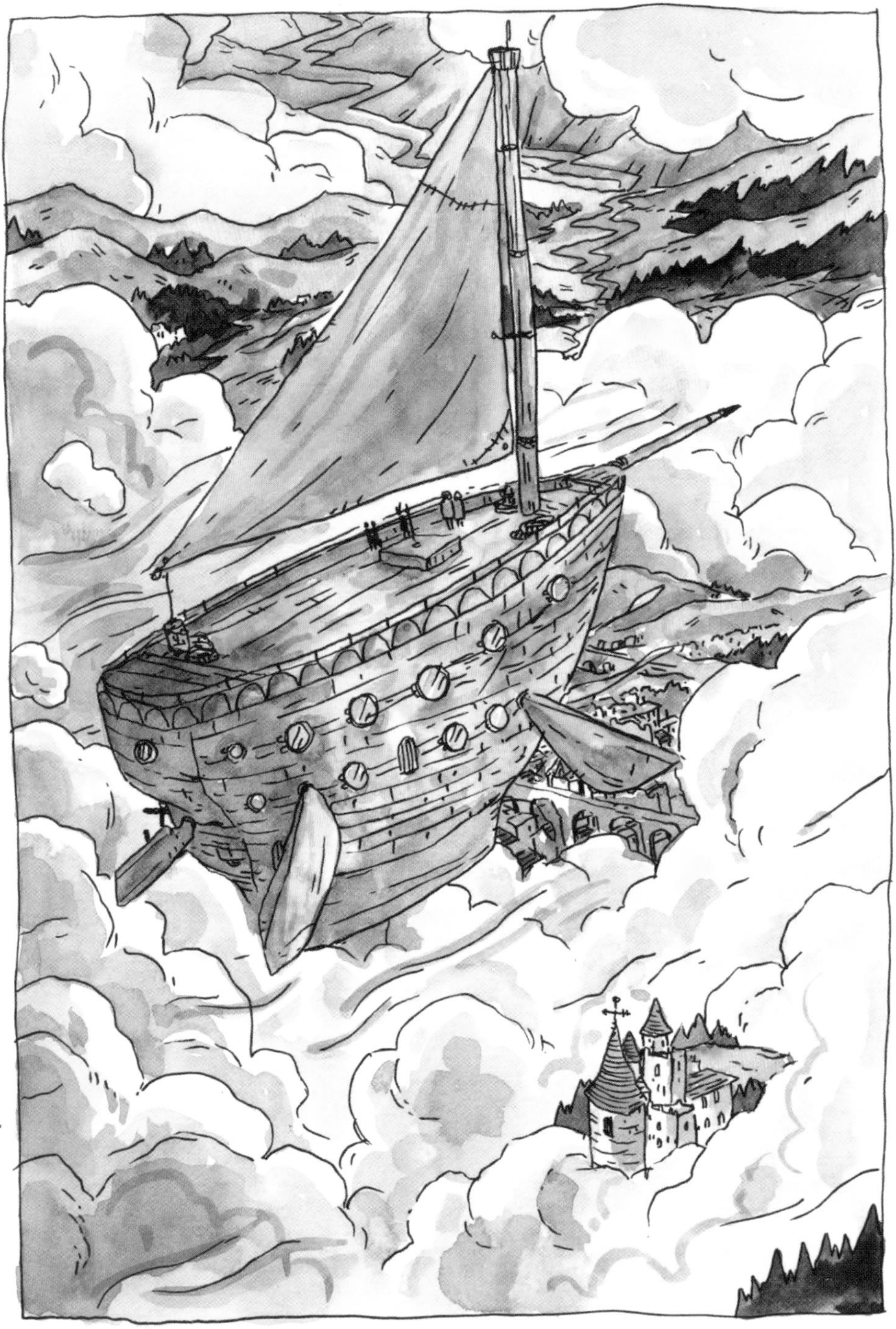

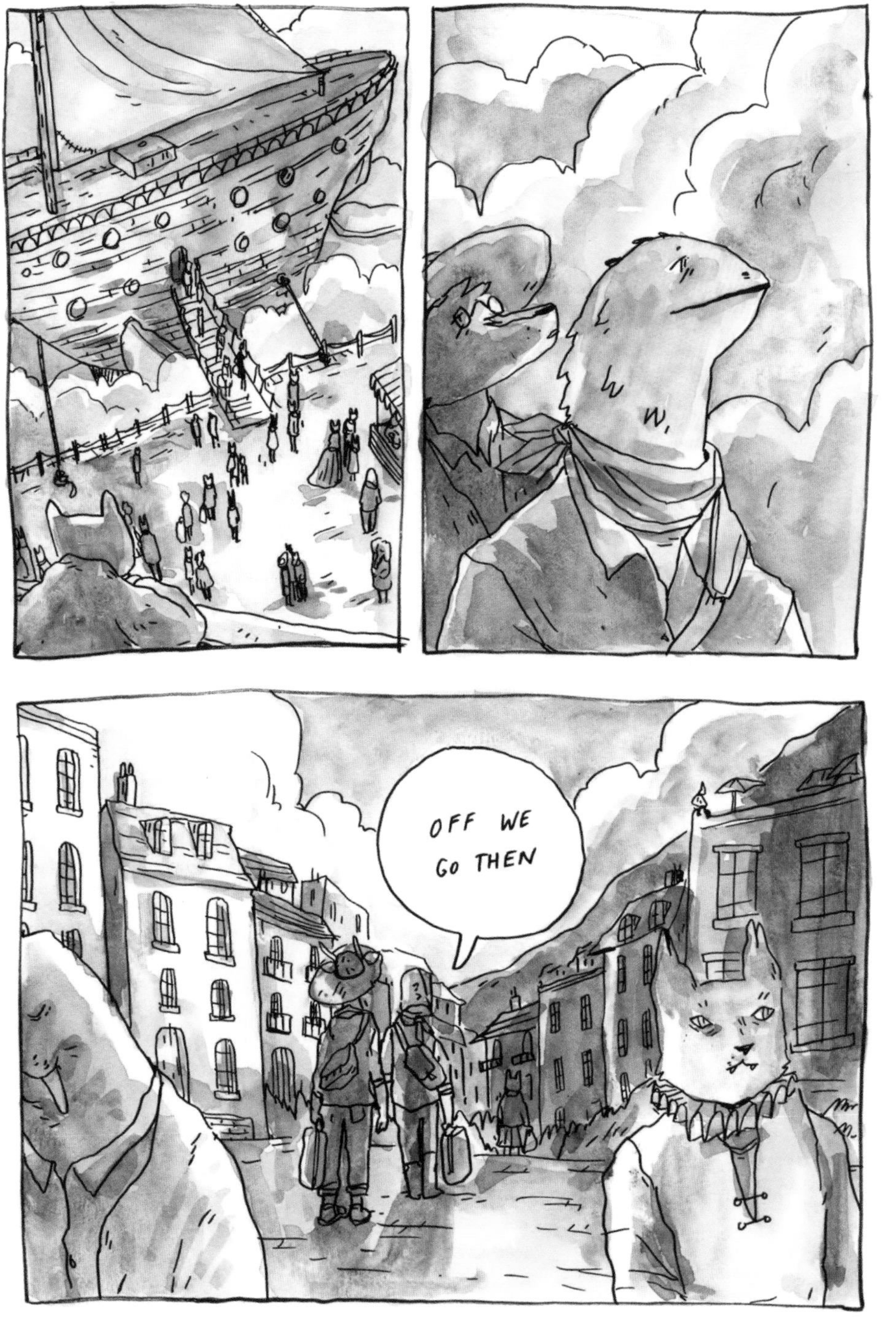
OFF WE GO THEN

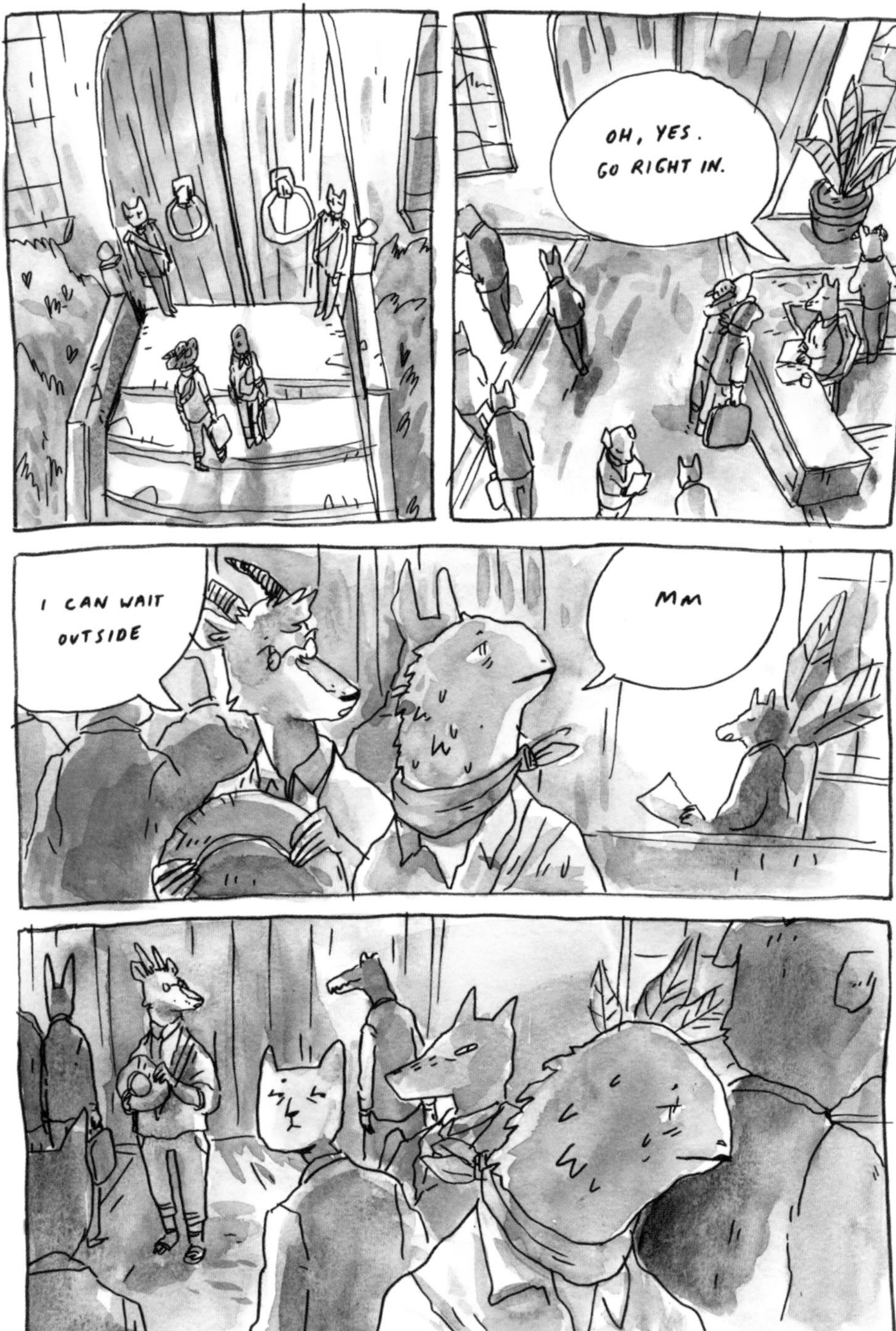
OH, YES.
GO RIGHT IN.
I CAN WAIT OUTSIDE
MM

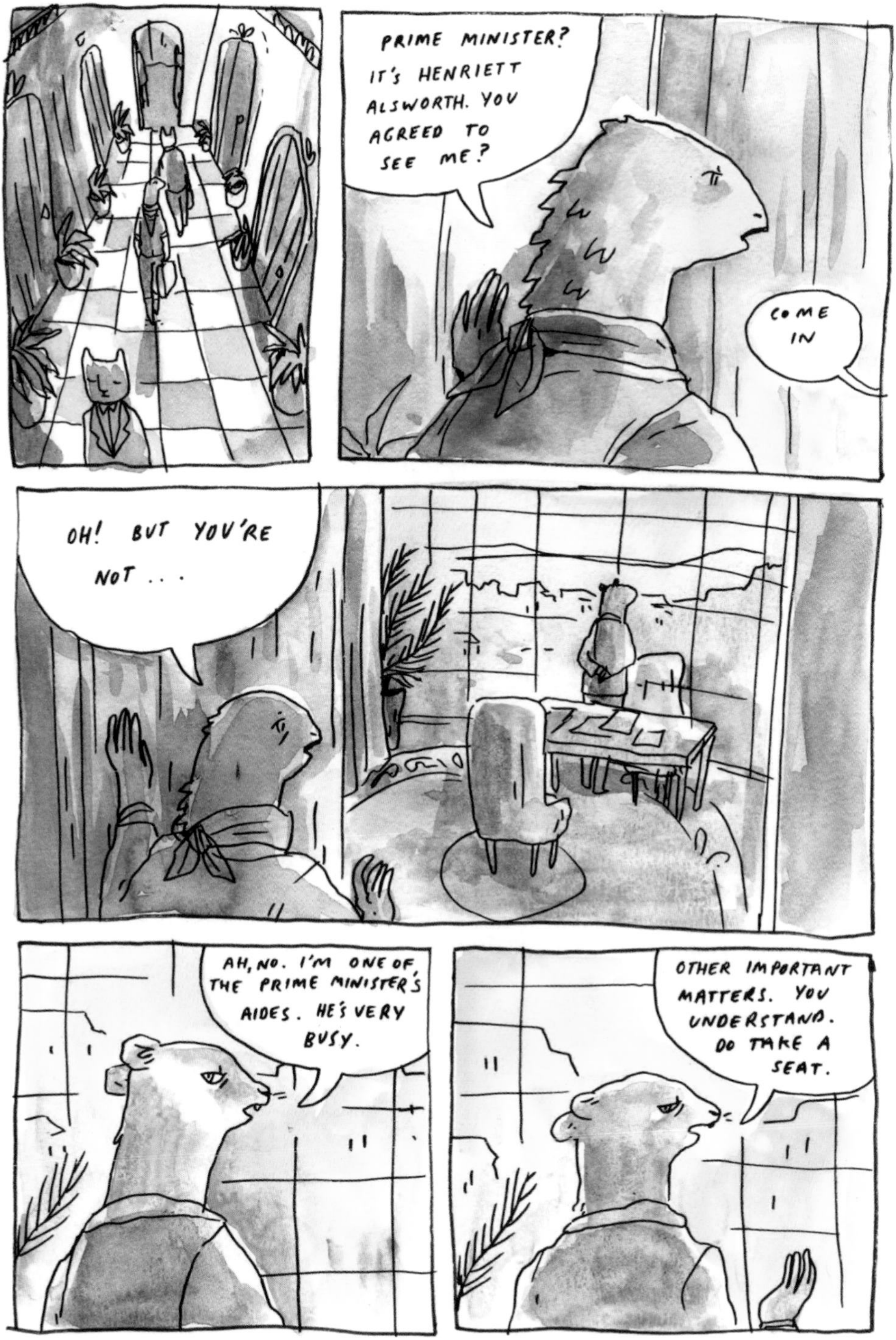
PRIME MINISTER? IT'S HENRIETT ALSWORTH. YOU AGREED TO SEE ME?
COME IN
OH! BUT YOU'RE NOT . . .
AH, NO. I'M ONE OF THE PRIME MINISTER'S AIDES. HE'S VERY BUSY.
OTHER IMPORTANT MATTERS. YOU UNDERSTAND. DO TAKE A SEAT.

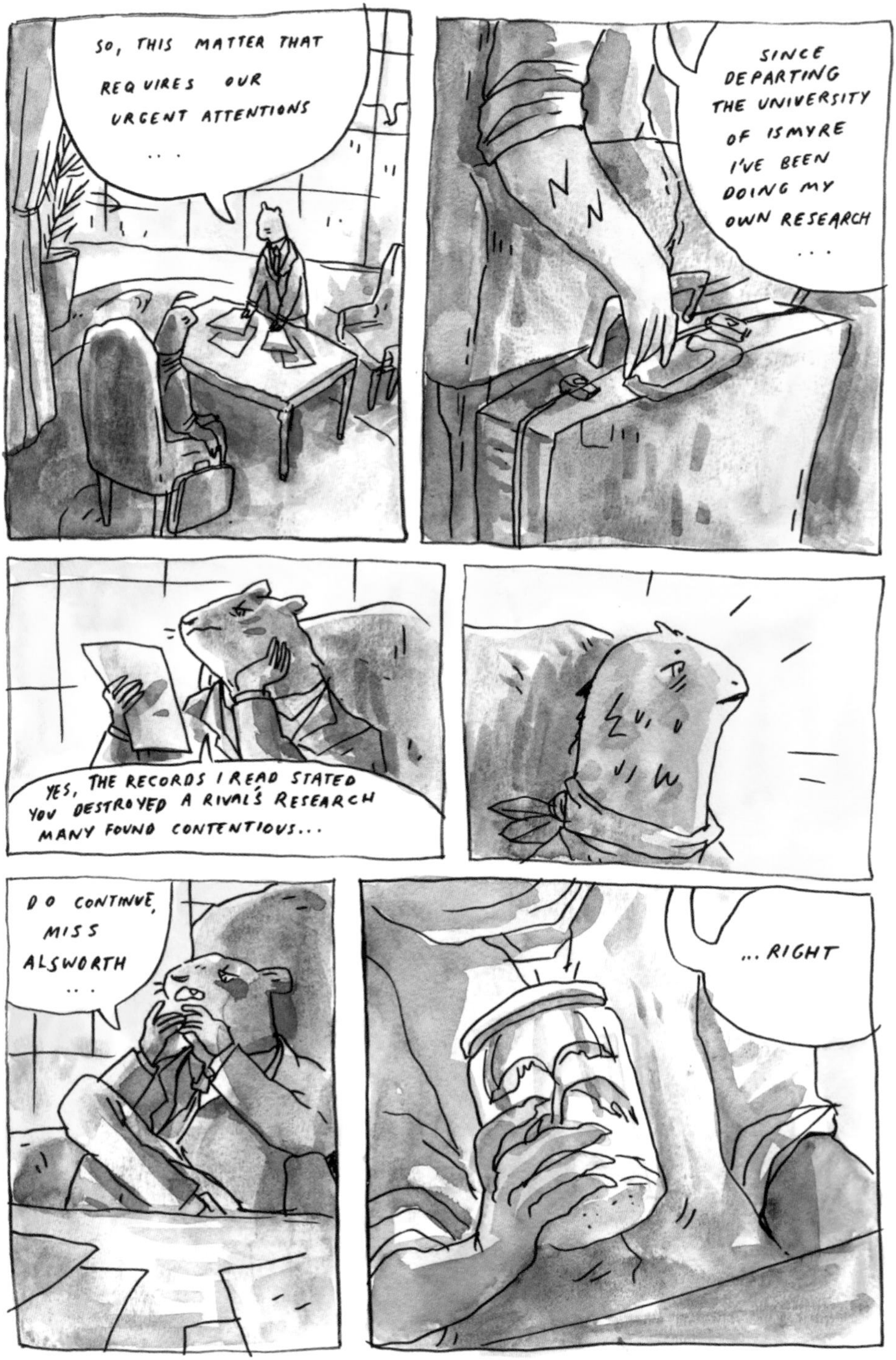
SO, THIS MATTER THAT REQUIRES OUR URGENT ATTENTIONS . . .
SINCE DEPARTING THE UNIVERSITY OF ISMYRE I'VE BEEN DOING MY OWN RESEARCH . . .
YES, THE RECORDS I READ STATED YOU DESTROYED A RIVAL'S RESEARCH MANY FOUND CONTENTIOUS...
DO CONTINUE, MISS ALSWORTH . . .
...RIGHT

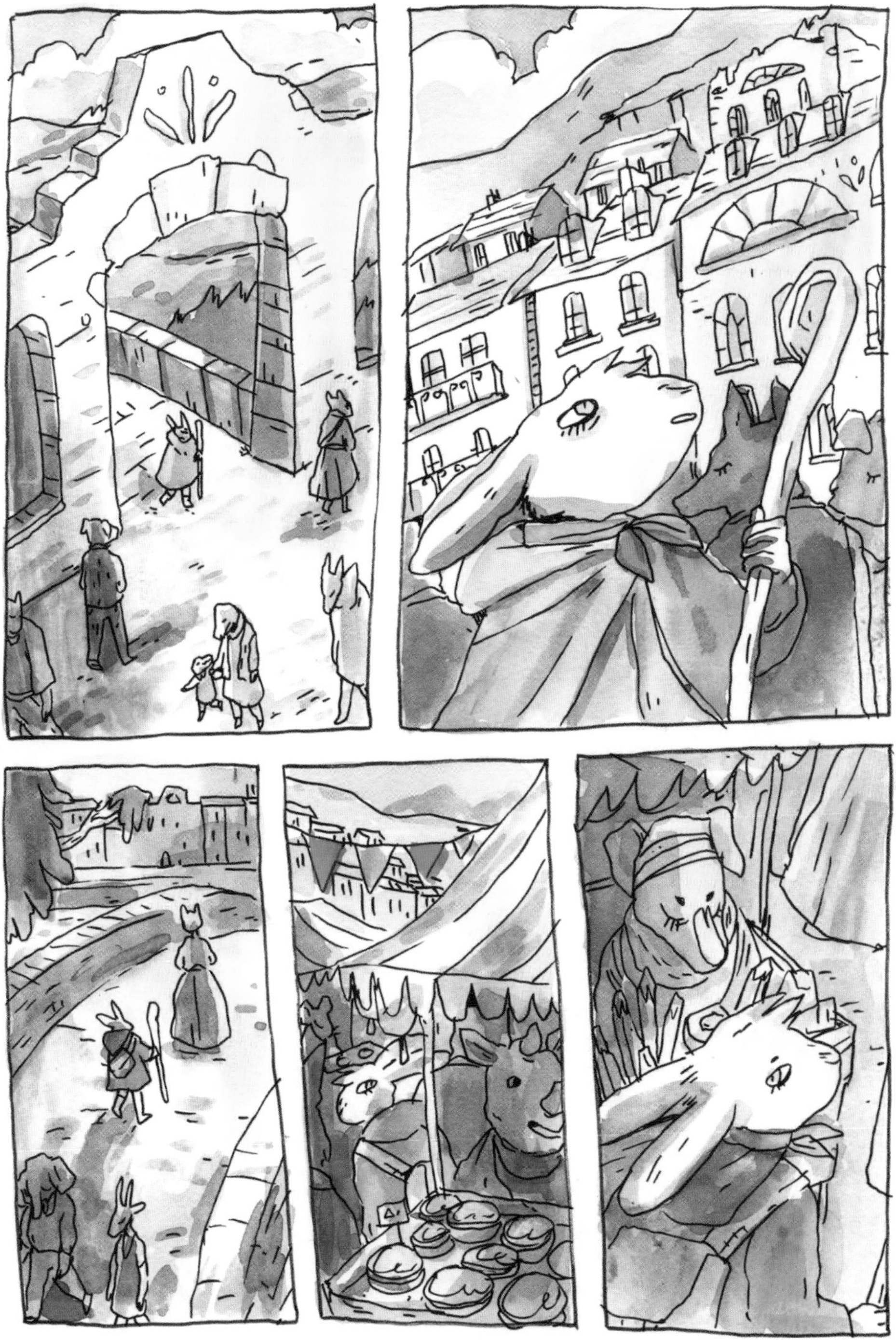

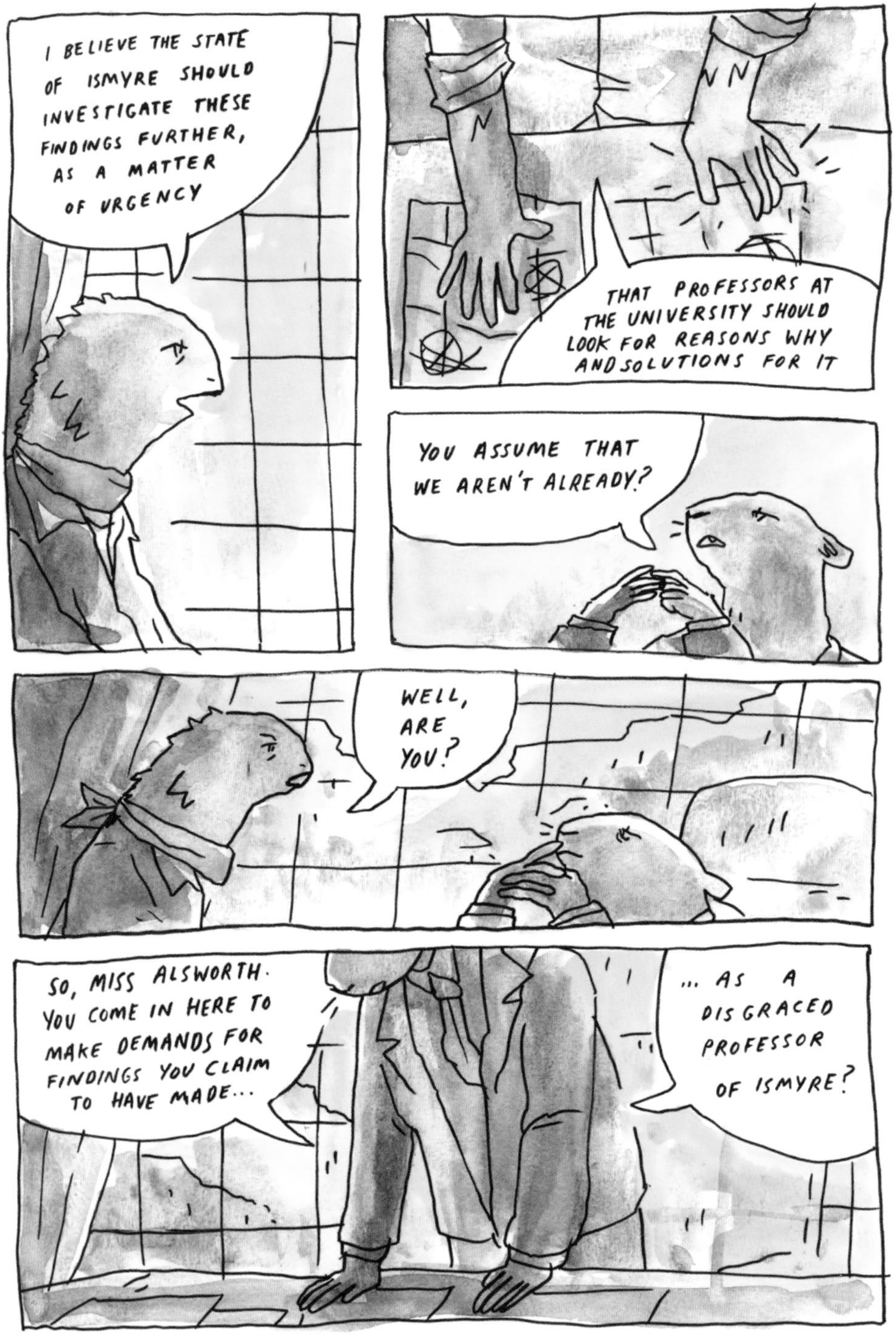
I BELIEVE THE STATE OF ISMYRE SHOULD INVESTIGATE THESE FINDINGS FURTHER, AS A MATTER OF URGENCY
THAT PROFESSORS AT THE UNIVERSITY SHOULD LOOK FOR REASONS WHY AND SOLUTIONS FOR IT
YOU ASSUME THAT WE AREN'T ALREADY?
WELL, ARE YOU?
SO, MISS ALSWORTH. YOU COME IN HERE TO MAKE DEMANDS FOR FINDINGS YOU CLAIM TO HAVE MADE...
... AS A DISGRACED PROFESSOR OF ISMYRE?

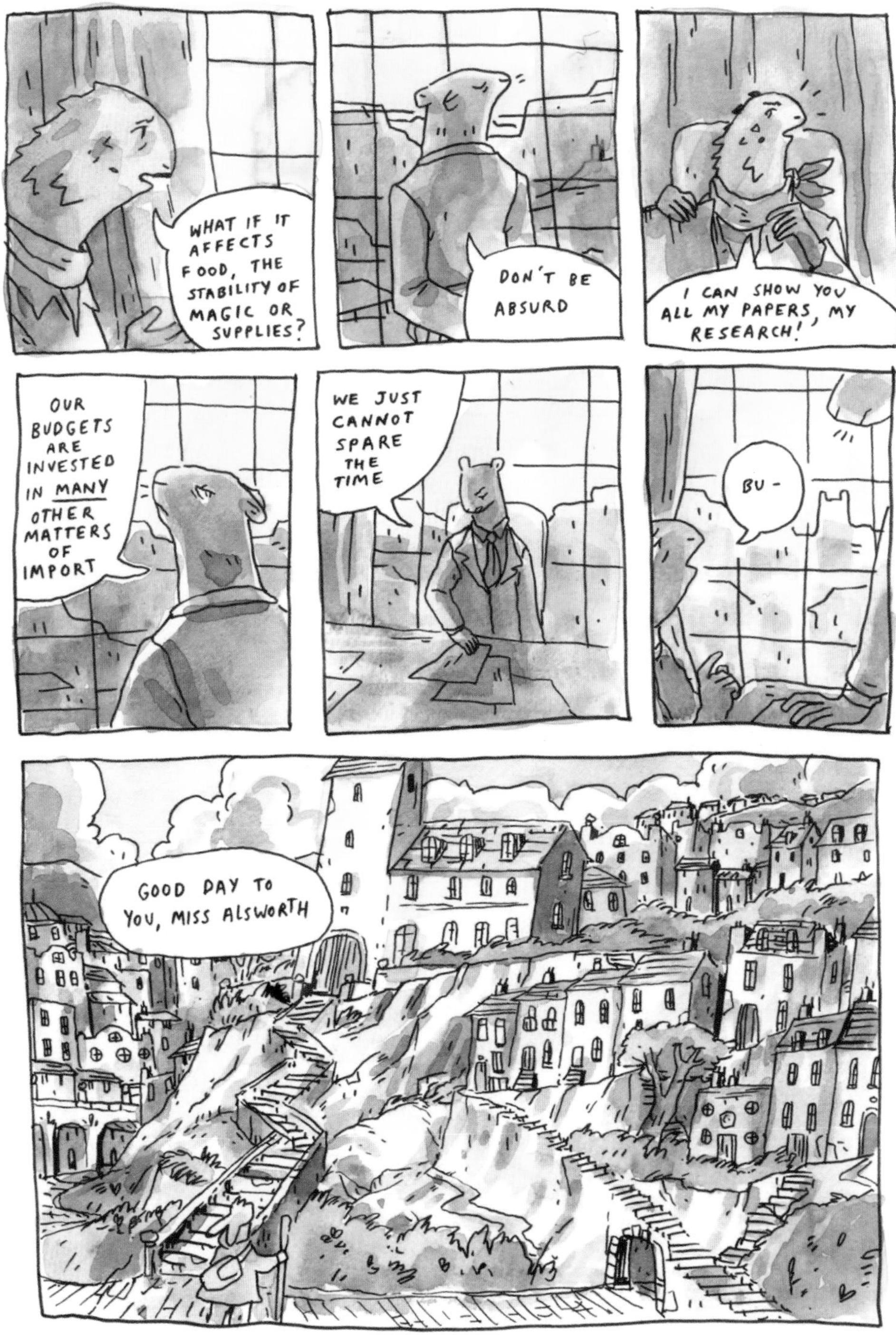
WHAT IF IT AFFECTS FOOD, THE STABILITY OF MAGIC OR SUPPLIES?
DON'T BE ABSURD
I CAN SHOW YOU ALL MY PAPERS, MY RESEARCH!
OUR BUDGETS ARE INVESTED IN MANY OTHER MATTERS OF IMPORT
WE JUST CANNOT SPARE THE TIME
BU -
GOOD DAY TO YOU, MISS ALSWORTH

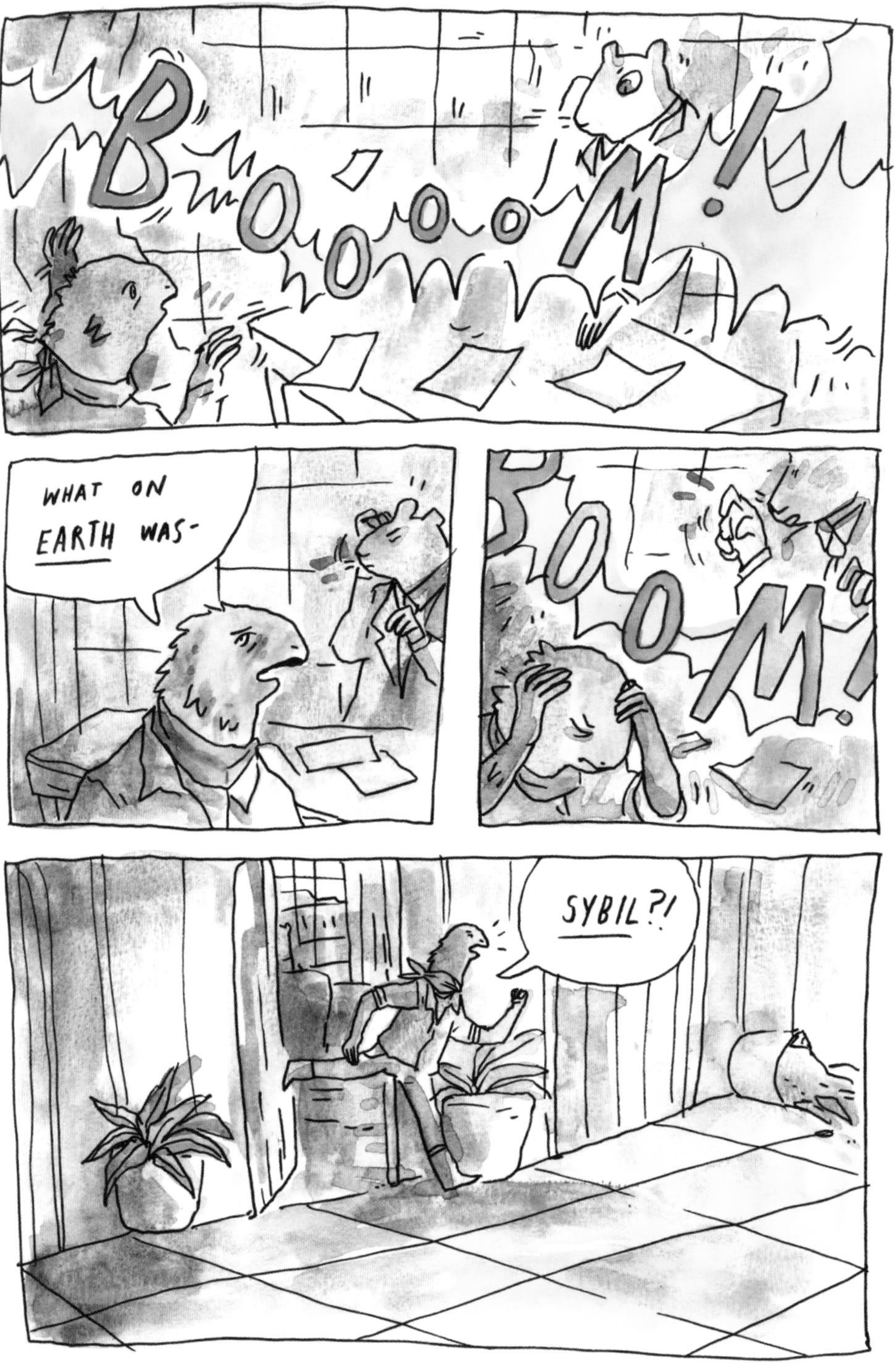
BOOoooM!
WHAT ON EARTH WAS-
BOOM!
SYBIL?!

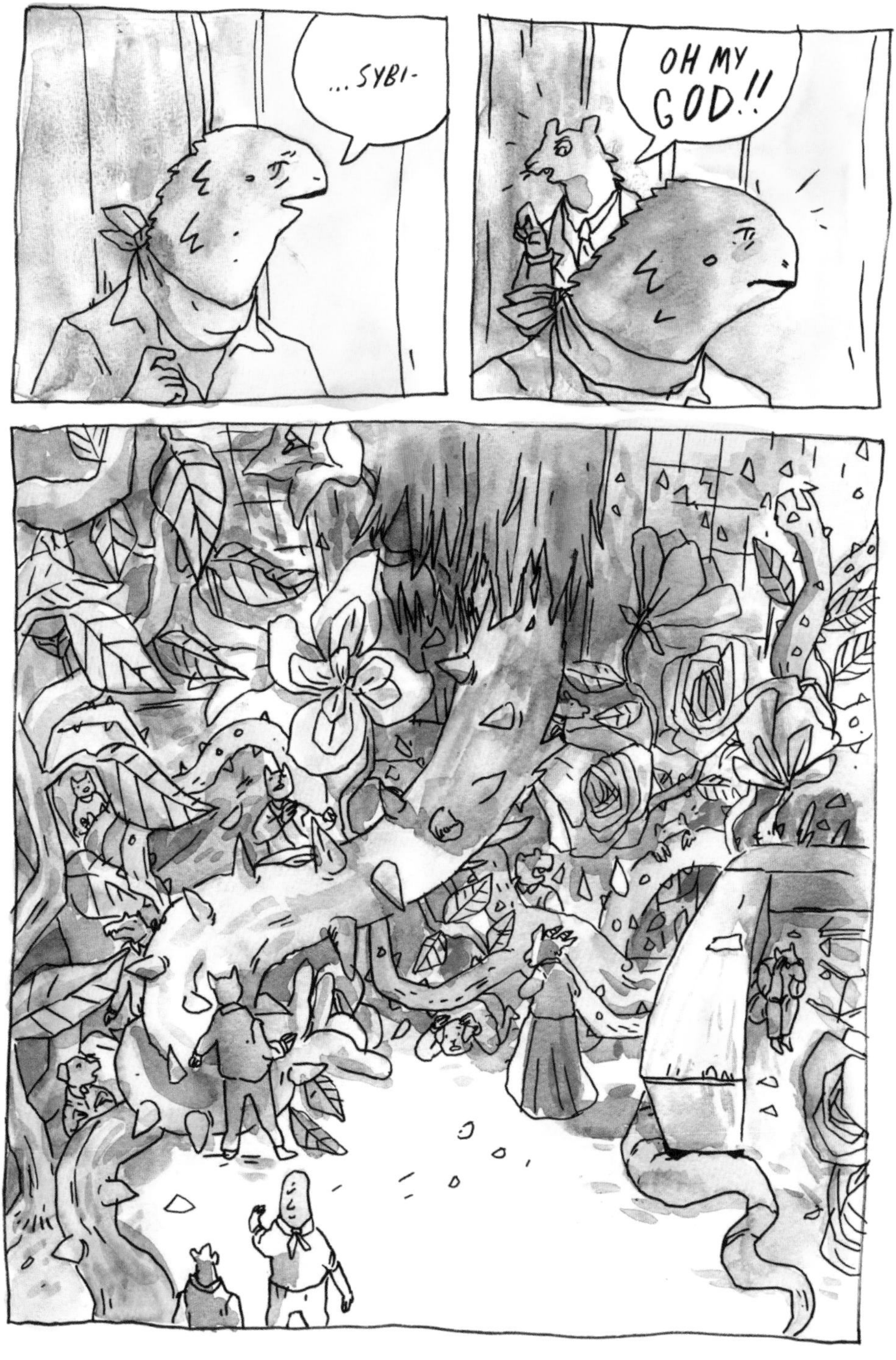
...SYBI-
OH MY GOD!!

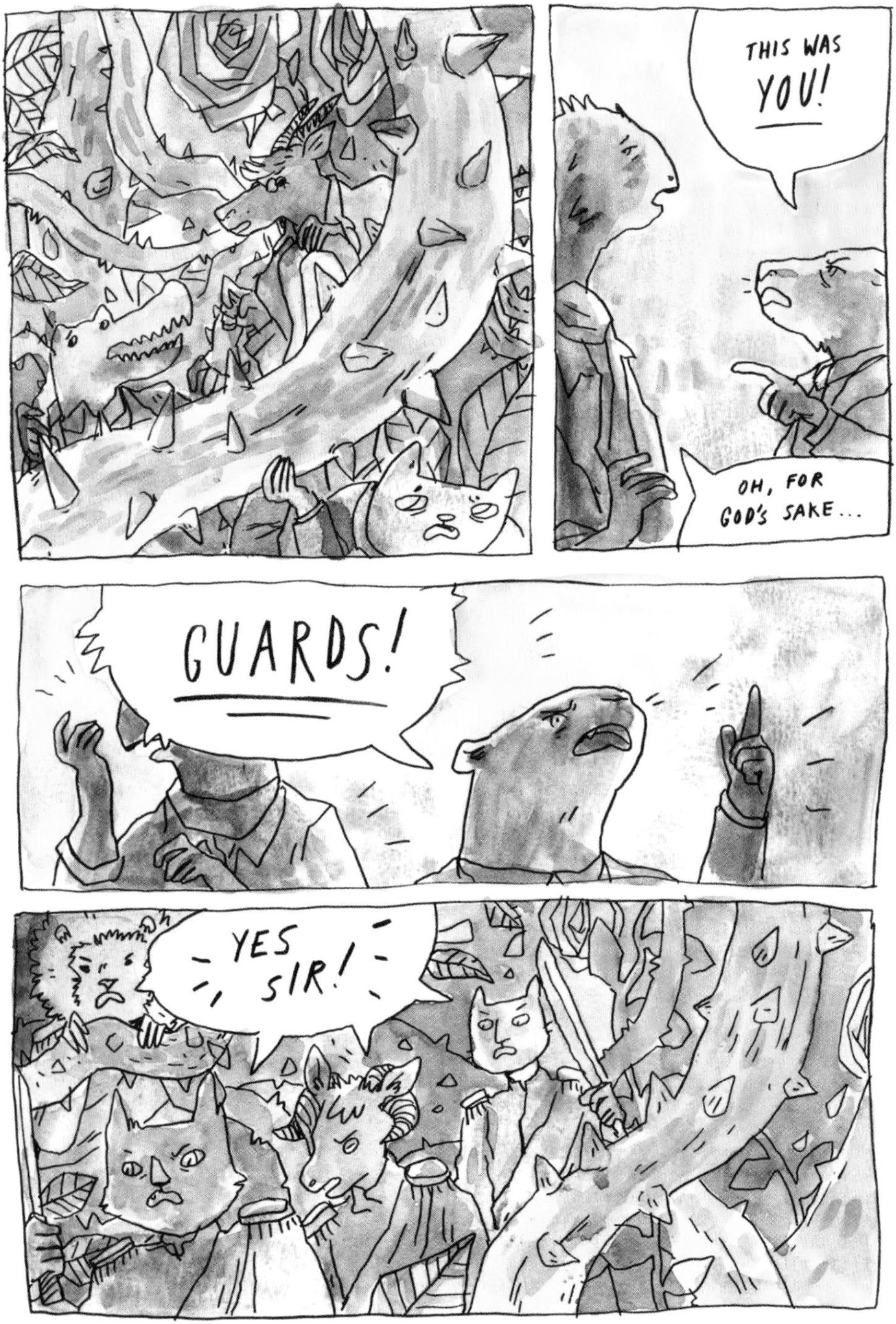
THIS WAS YOU!
OH, FOR GOD'S SAKE...
GUARDS!
YES SIR!

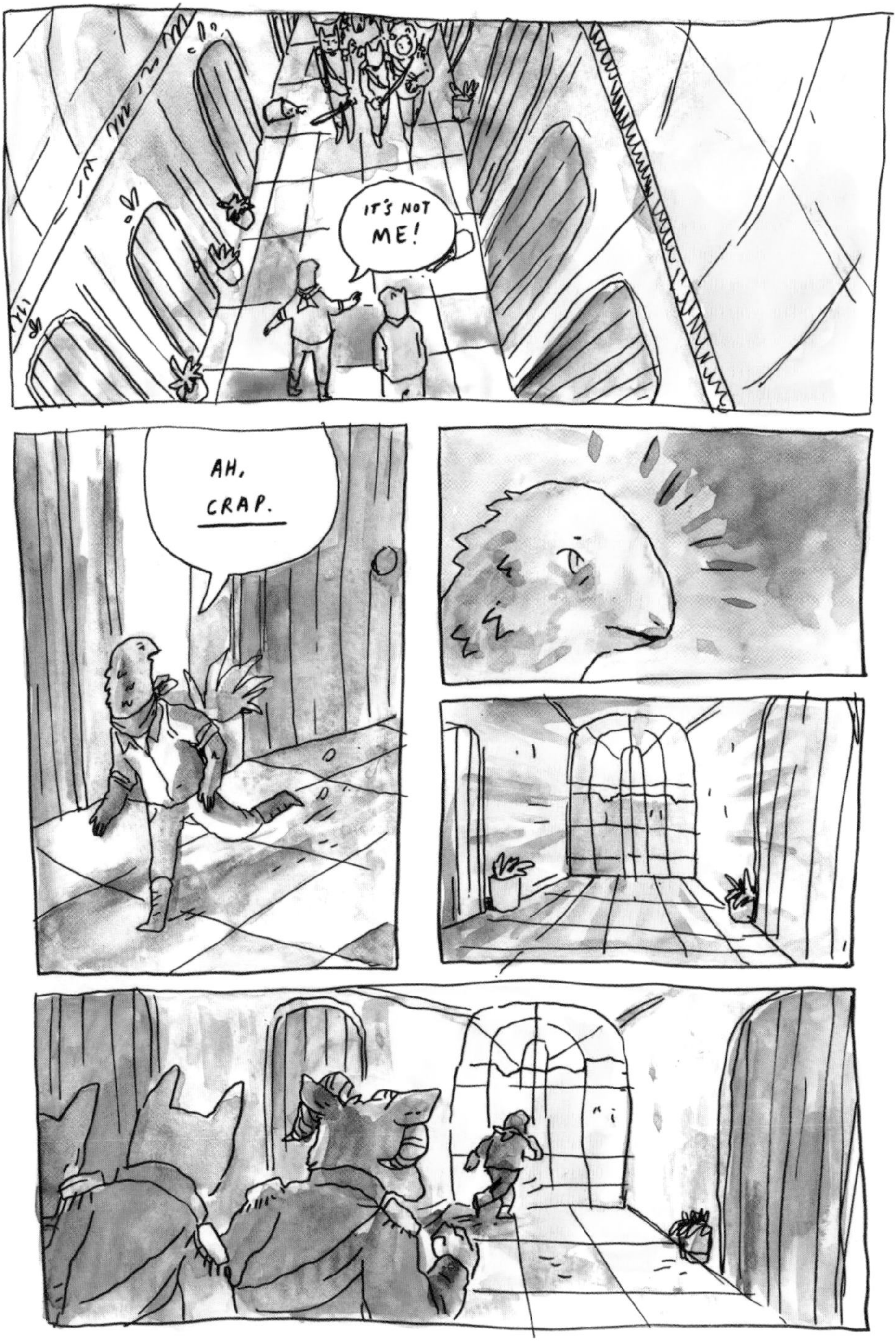
IT'S NOT ME!
AH, CRAP.

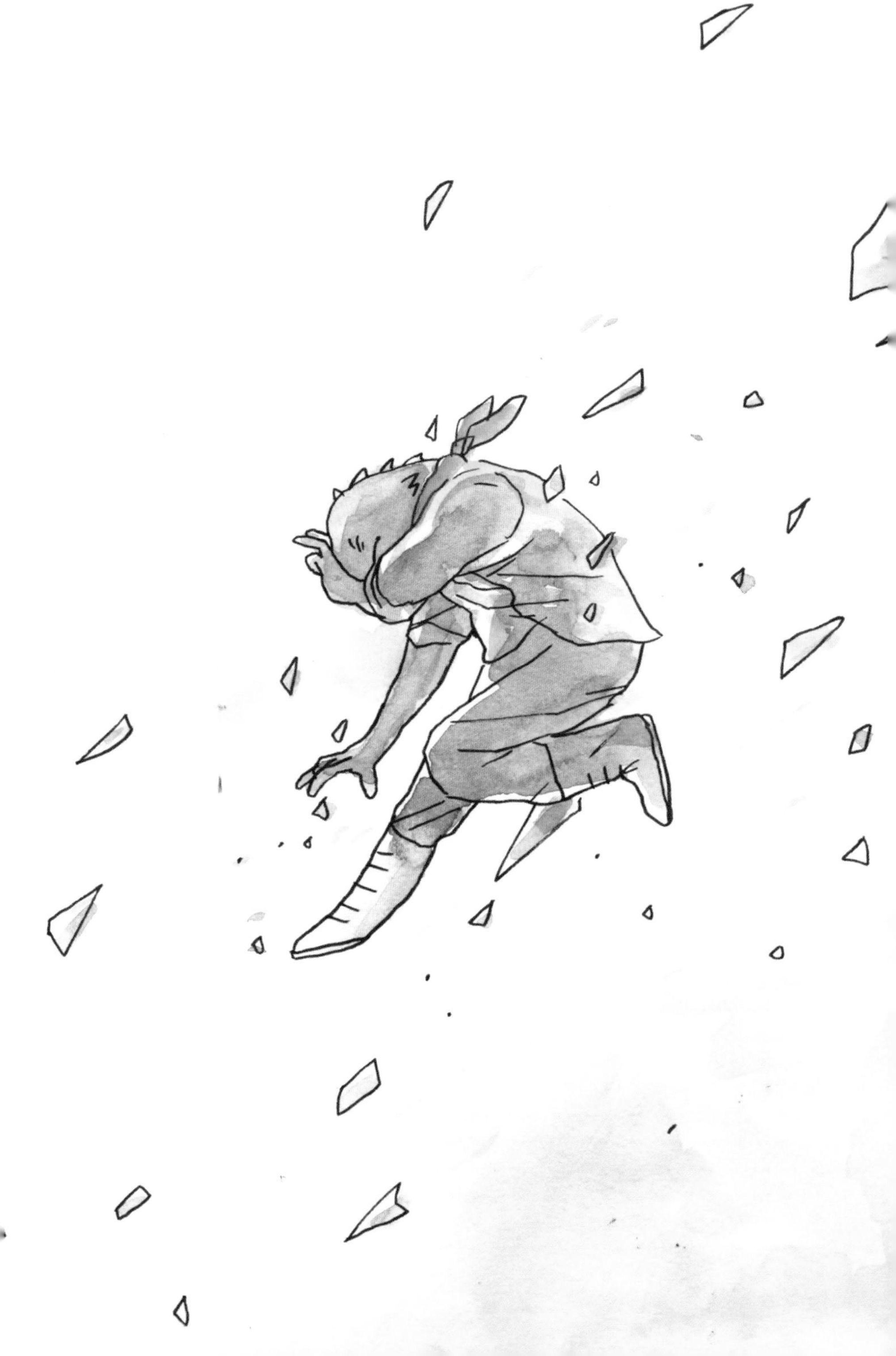

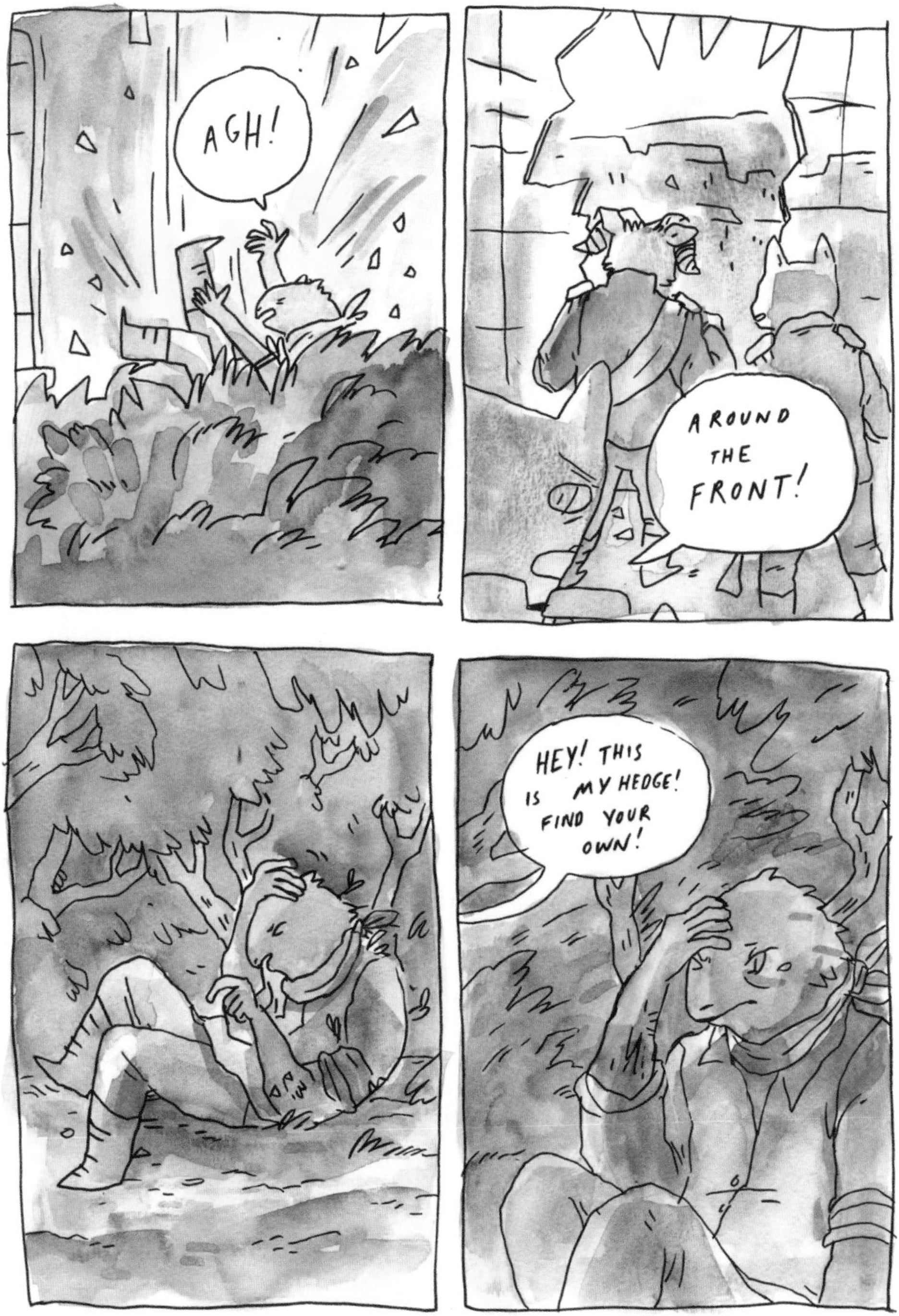
AGH!
AROUND THE FRONT!
HEY! THIS IS MY HEDGE! FIND YOUR OWN!

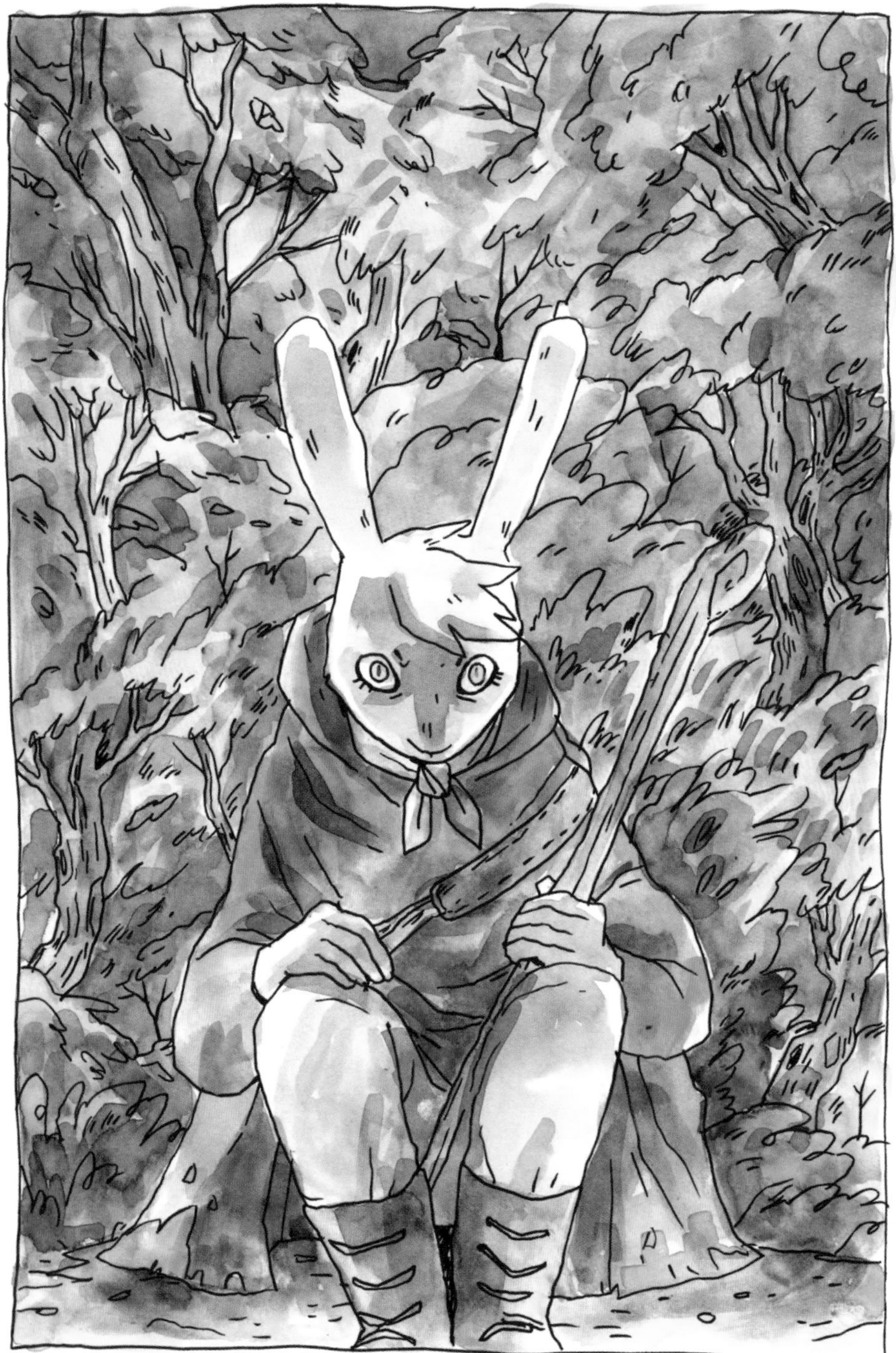

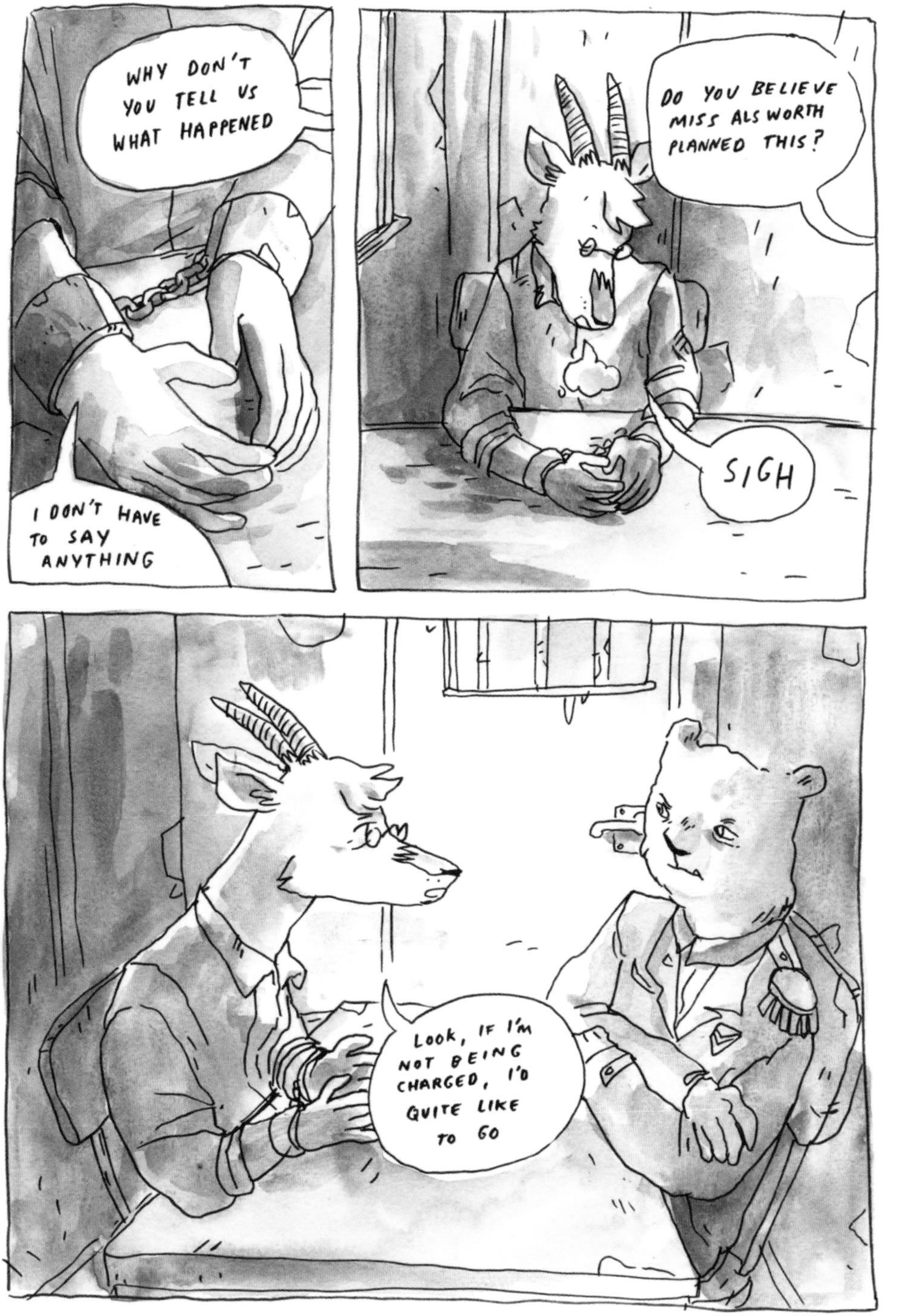
WHY DON'T YOU TELL US WHAT HAPPENED
I DON'T HAVE TO SAY ANYTHING
DO YOU BELIEVE MISS ALSWORTH PLANNED THIS?
SIGH
LOOK, IF I'M NOT BEING CHARGED, I'D QUITE LIKE TO GO

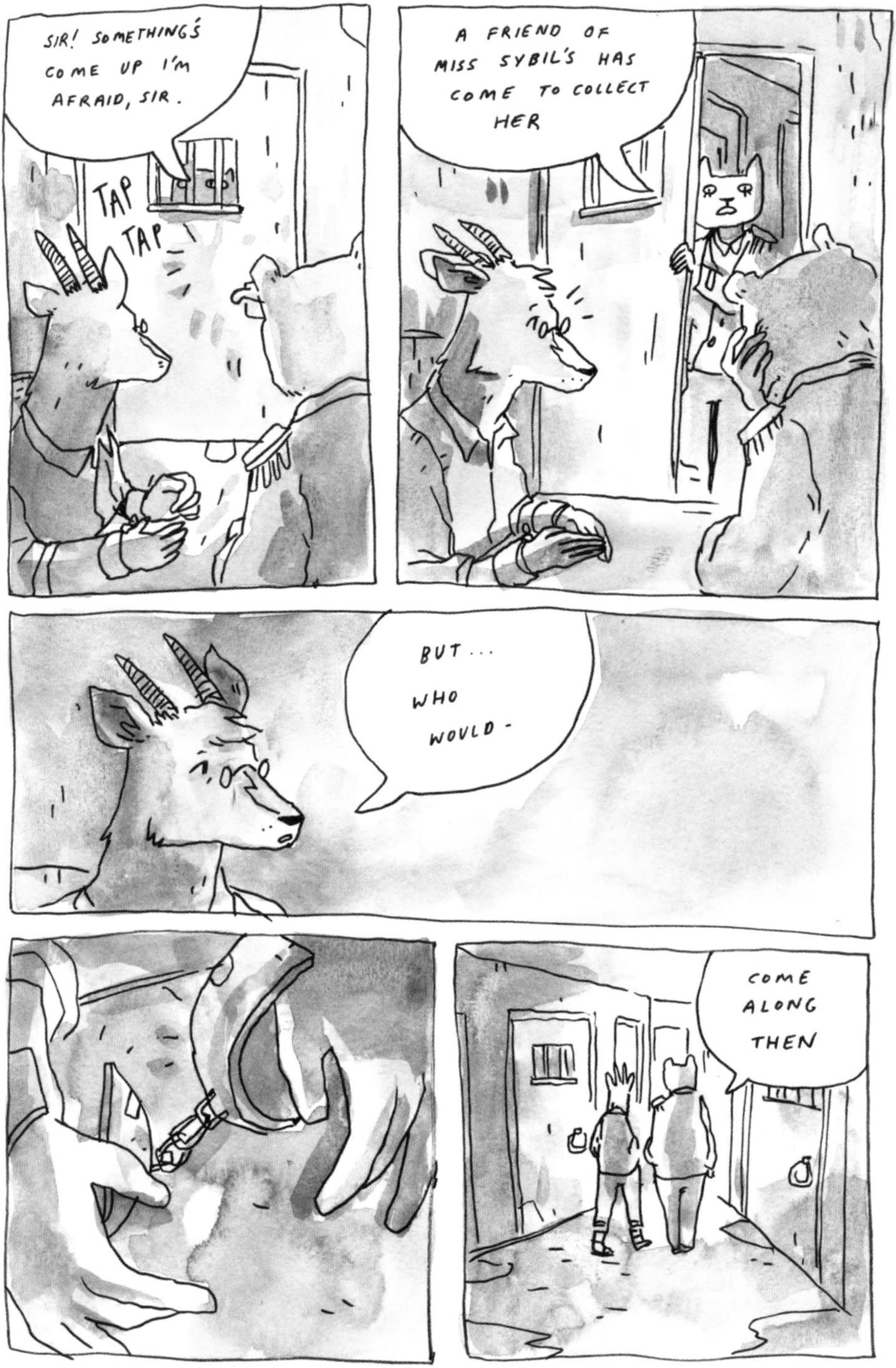
SIR! SOMETHING'S COME UP I'M AFRAID, SIR.
TAP TAP
A FRIEND OF MISS SYBIL'S HAS COME TO COLLECT HER
BUT... WHO WOULD-
COME ALONG THEN

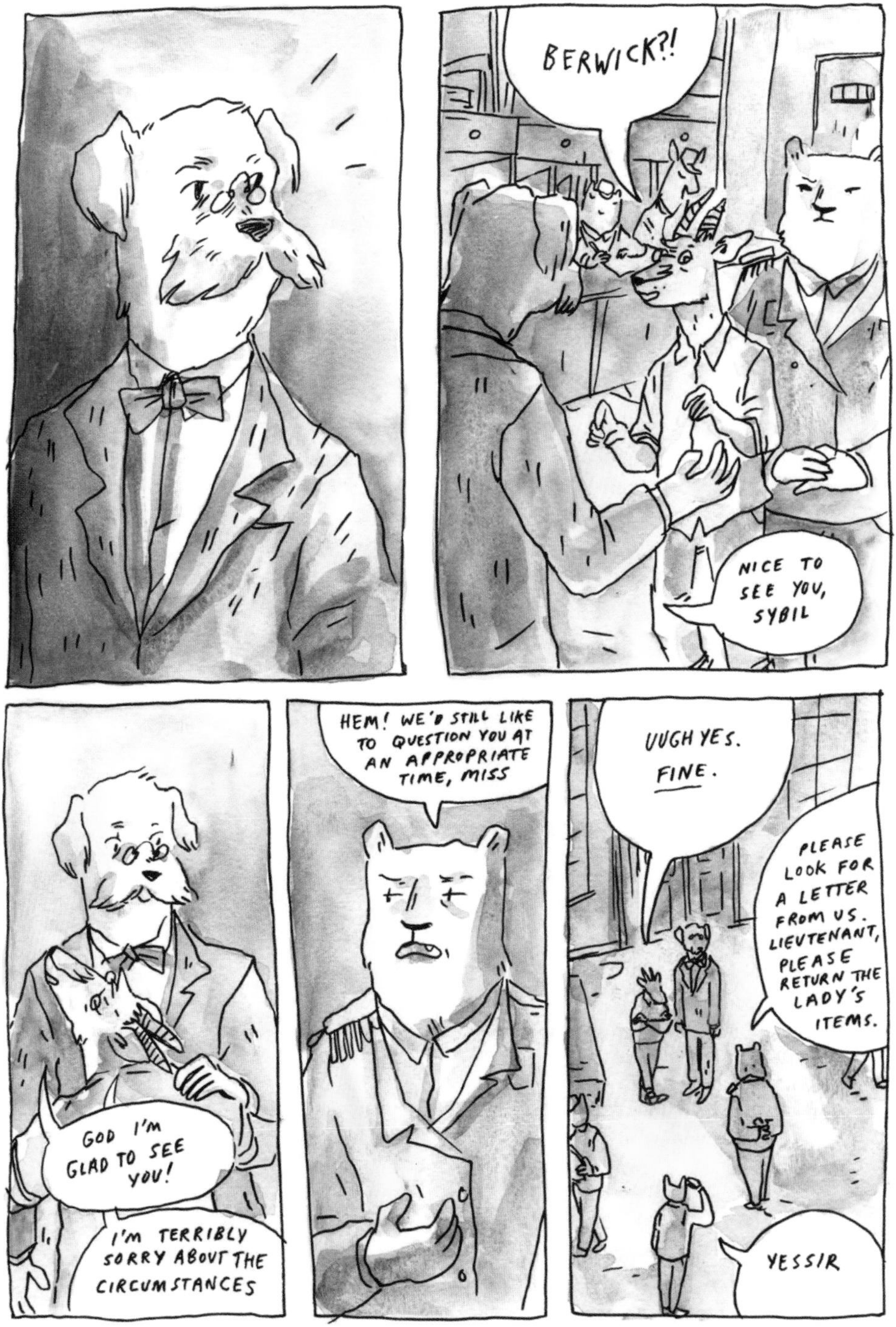
BERWICK?!
NICE TO SEE YOU, SYBIL
GOD I'M GLAD TO SEE YOU!
I'M TERRIBLY SORRY ABOUT THE CIRCUMSTANCES
HEM! WE'D STILL LIKE TO QUESTION YOU AT AN APPROPRIATE TIME, MISS
UUGH YES. FINE.
PLEASE LOOK FOR A LETTER FROM US. LIEUTENANT, PLEASE RETURN THE LADY'S ITEMS.
YESSIR

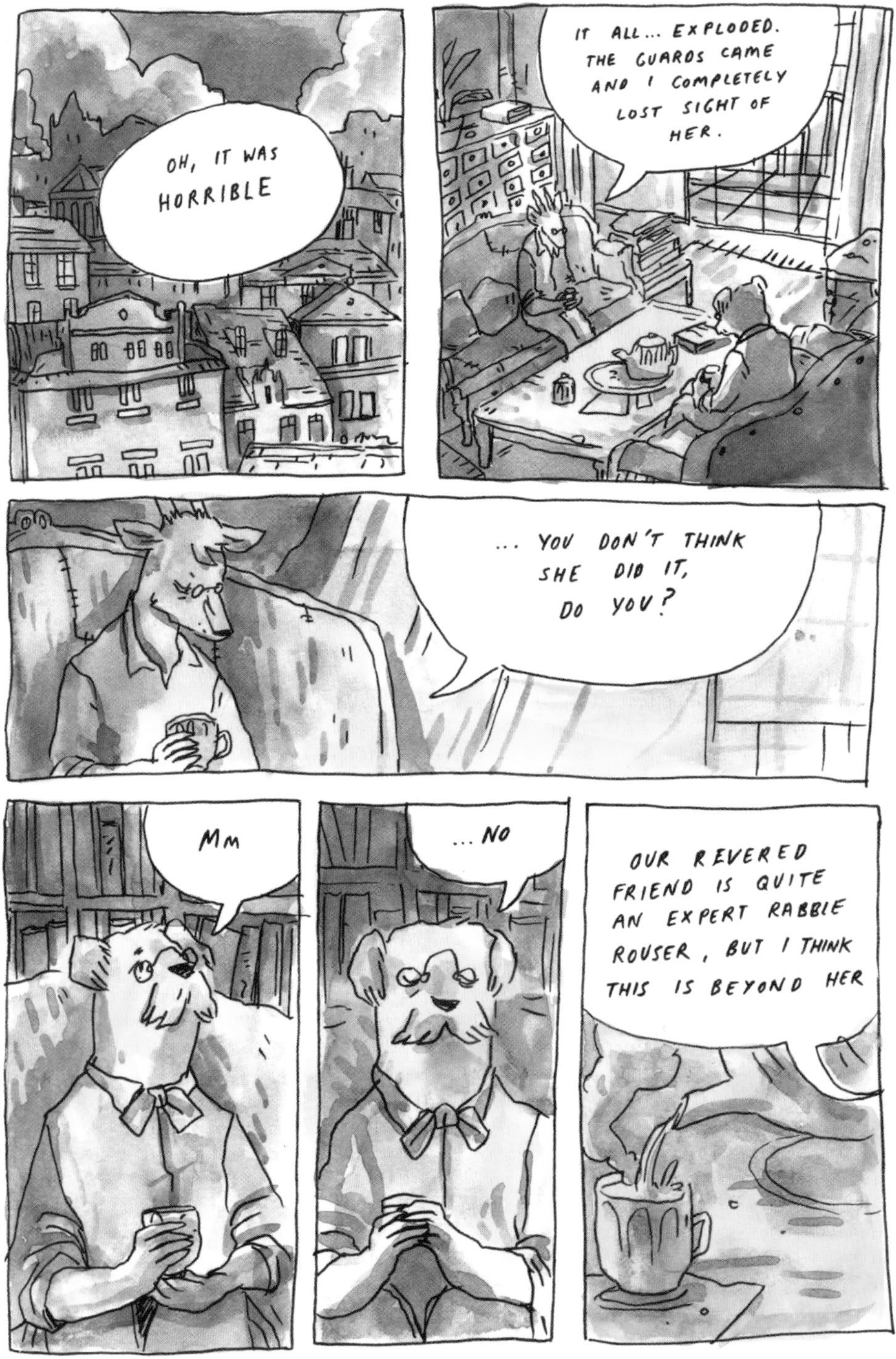
OH, IT WAS HORRIBLE
IT ALL... EXPLODED. THE GUARDS CAME AND I COMPLETELY LOST SIGHT OF HER.
... YOU DON'T THINK SHE DID IT, DO YOU?
Mm
...NO
OUR REVERED FRIEND IS QUITE AN EXPERT RABBLE ROUSER, BUT I THINK THIS IS BEYOND HER

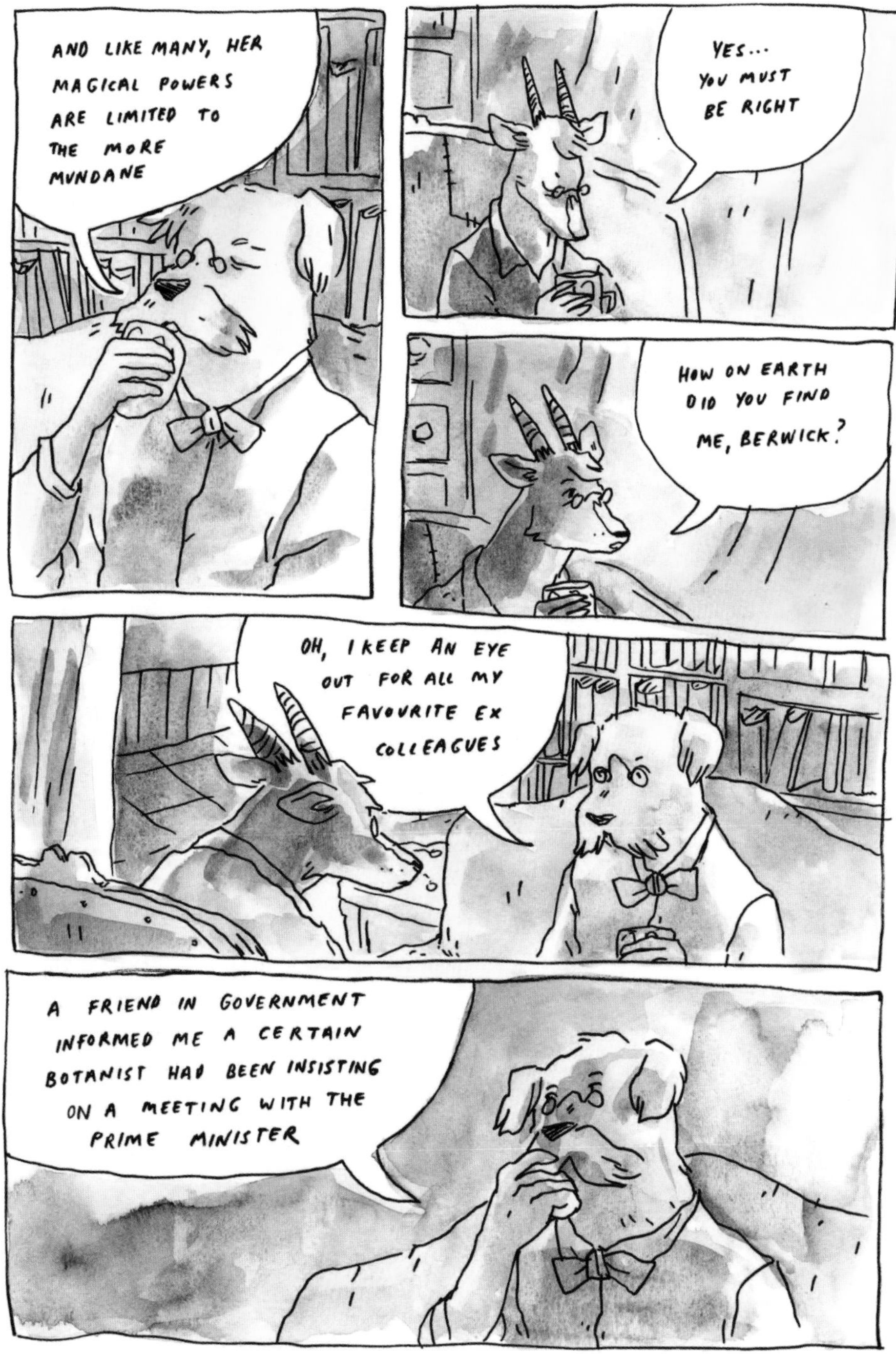
AND LIKE MANY, HER MAGICAL POWERS ARE LIMITED TO THE MORE MUNDANE
YES... YOU MUST BE RIGHT
HOW ON EARTH DID YOU FIND ME, BERWICK?
OH, I KEEP AN EYE OUT FOR ALL MY FAVOURITE EX COLLEAGUES
A FRIEND IN GOVERNMENT INFORMED ME A CERTAIN BOTANIST HAD BEEN INSISTING ON A MEETING WITH THE PRIME MINISTER

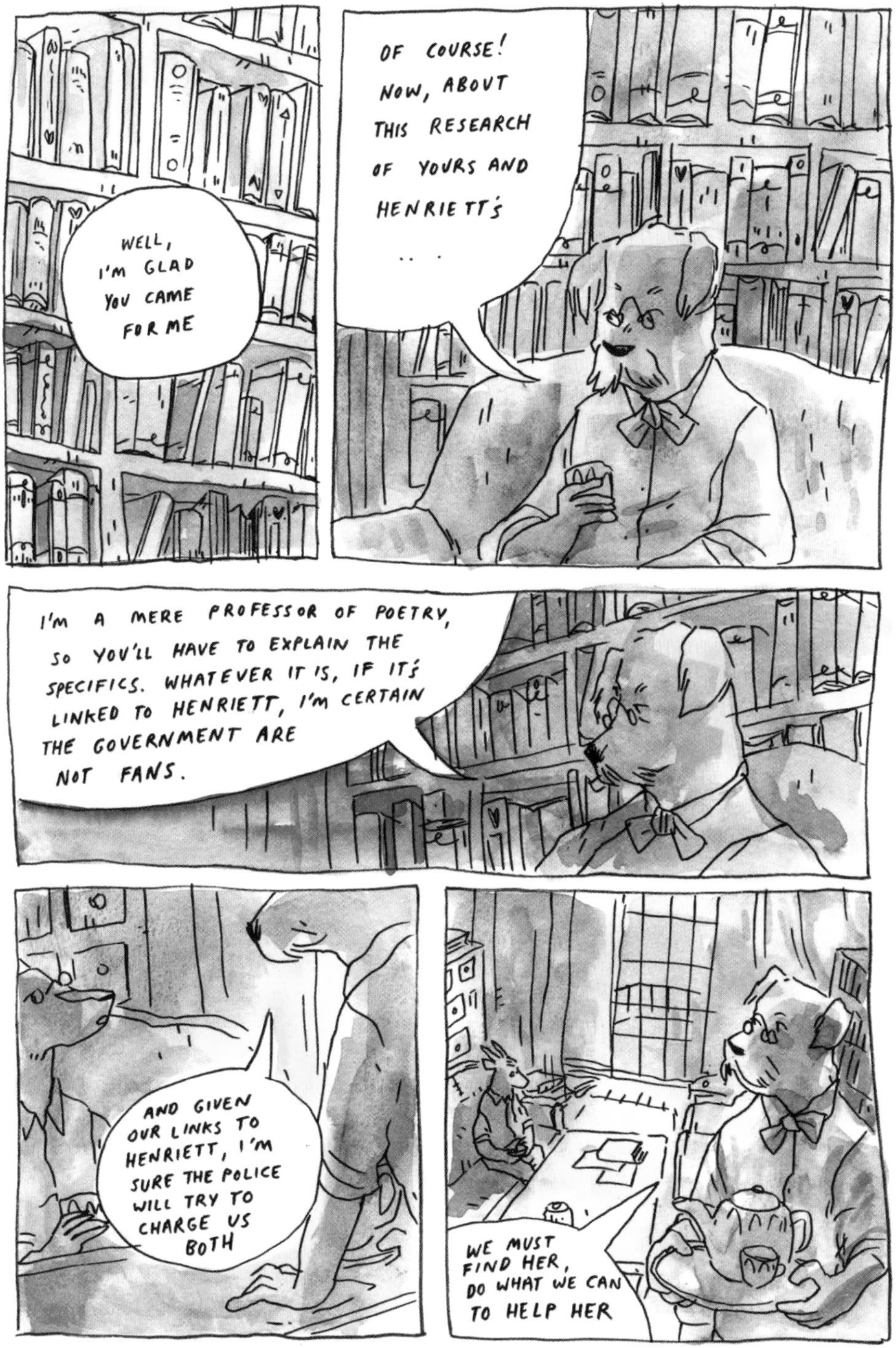

WELL, I'M GLAD YOU CAME FOR ME
OF COURSE! NOW, ABOUT THIS RESEARCH OF YOURS AND HENRIETT'S . . .
I'M A MERE PROFESSOR OF POETRY, SO YOU'LL HAVE TO EXPLAIN THE SPECIFICS. WHATEVER IT IS, IF IT'S LINKED TO HENRIETT, I'M CERTAIN THE GOVERNMENT ARE NOT FANS.
AND GIVEN OUR LINKS TO HENRIETT, I'M SURE THE POLICE WILL TRY TO CHARGE US BOTH
WE MUST FIND HER, DO WHAT WE CAN TO HELP HER

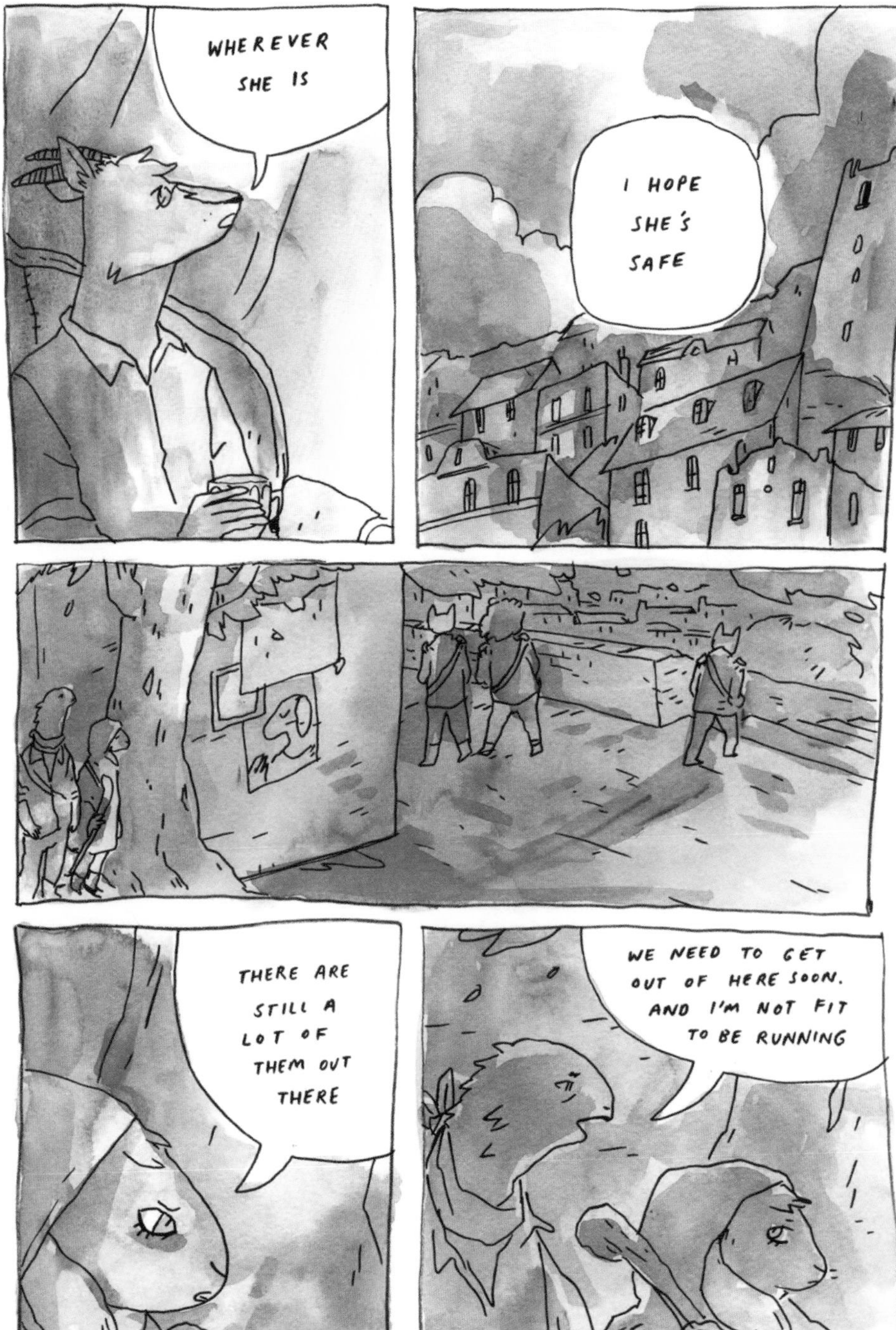
WHEREVER SHE IS
I HOPE SHE'S SAFE
THERE ARE STILL A LOT OF THEM OUT THERE
WE NEED TO GET OUT OF HERE SOON. AND I'M NOT FIT TO BE RUNNING

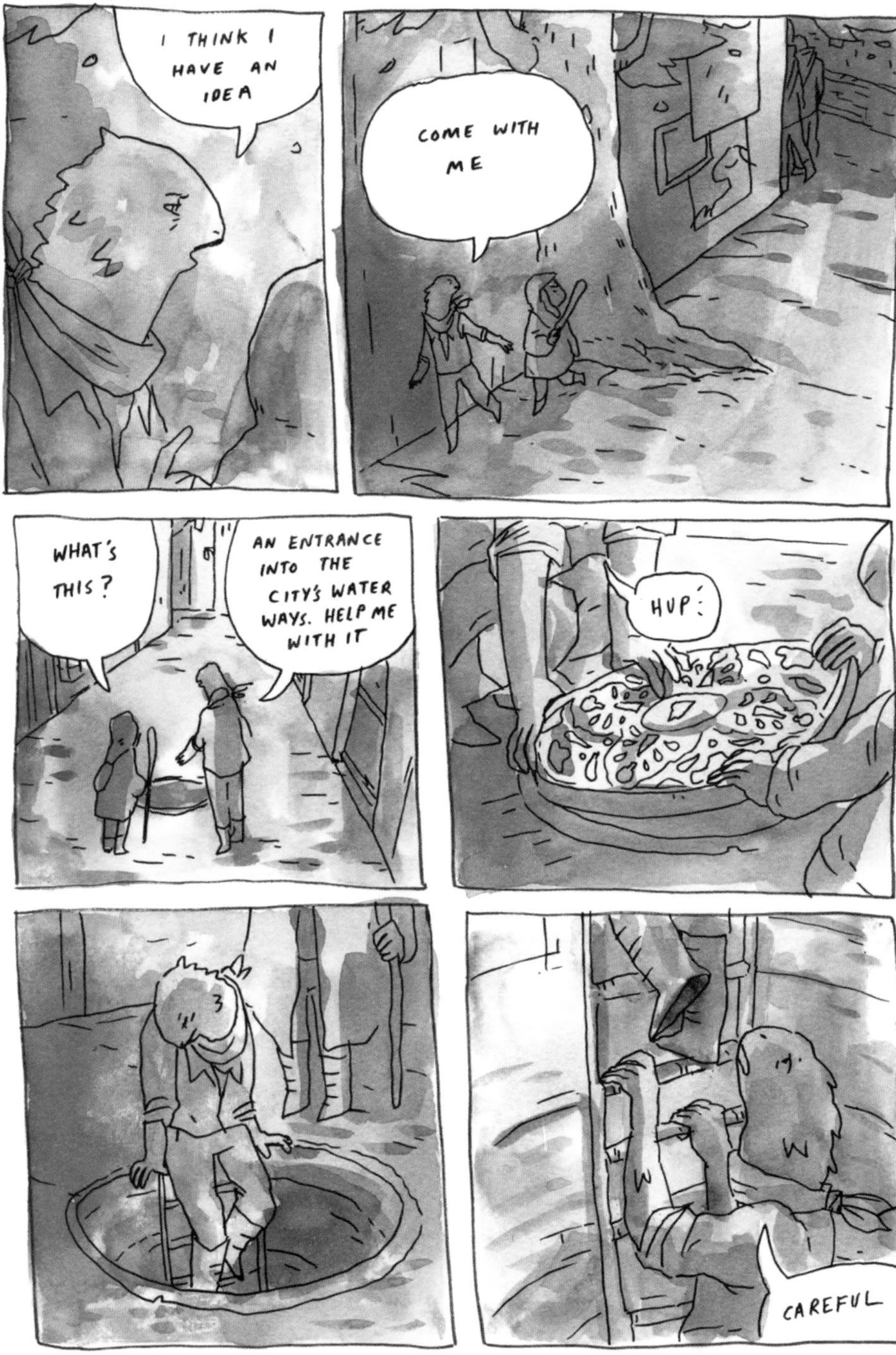
I THINK I HAVE AN IDEA
COME WITH ME
WHAT'S THIS?
AN ENTRANCE INTO THE CITY'S WATER WAYS. HELP ME WITH IT
HUP!
CAREFUL

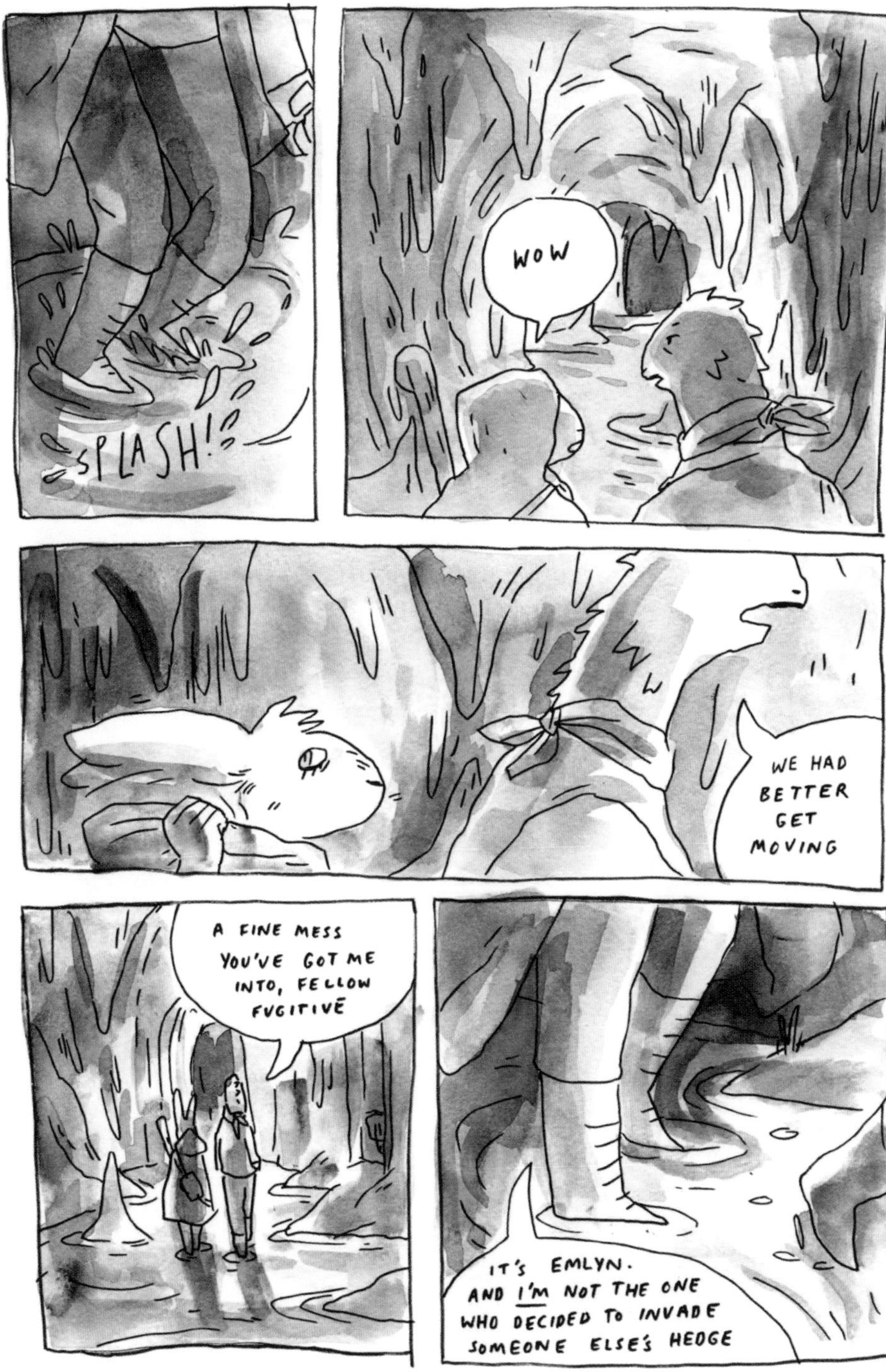
SPLASH!
WOW
WE HAD BETTER GET MOVING
A FINE MESS YOU'VE GOT ME INTO, FELLOW FUGITIVE
IT'S EMLYN.
AND I'M NOT THE ONE WHO DECIDED TO INVADE SOMEONE ELSE'S HEDGE

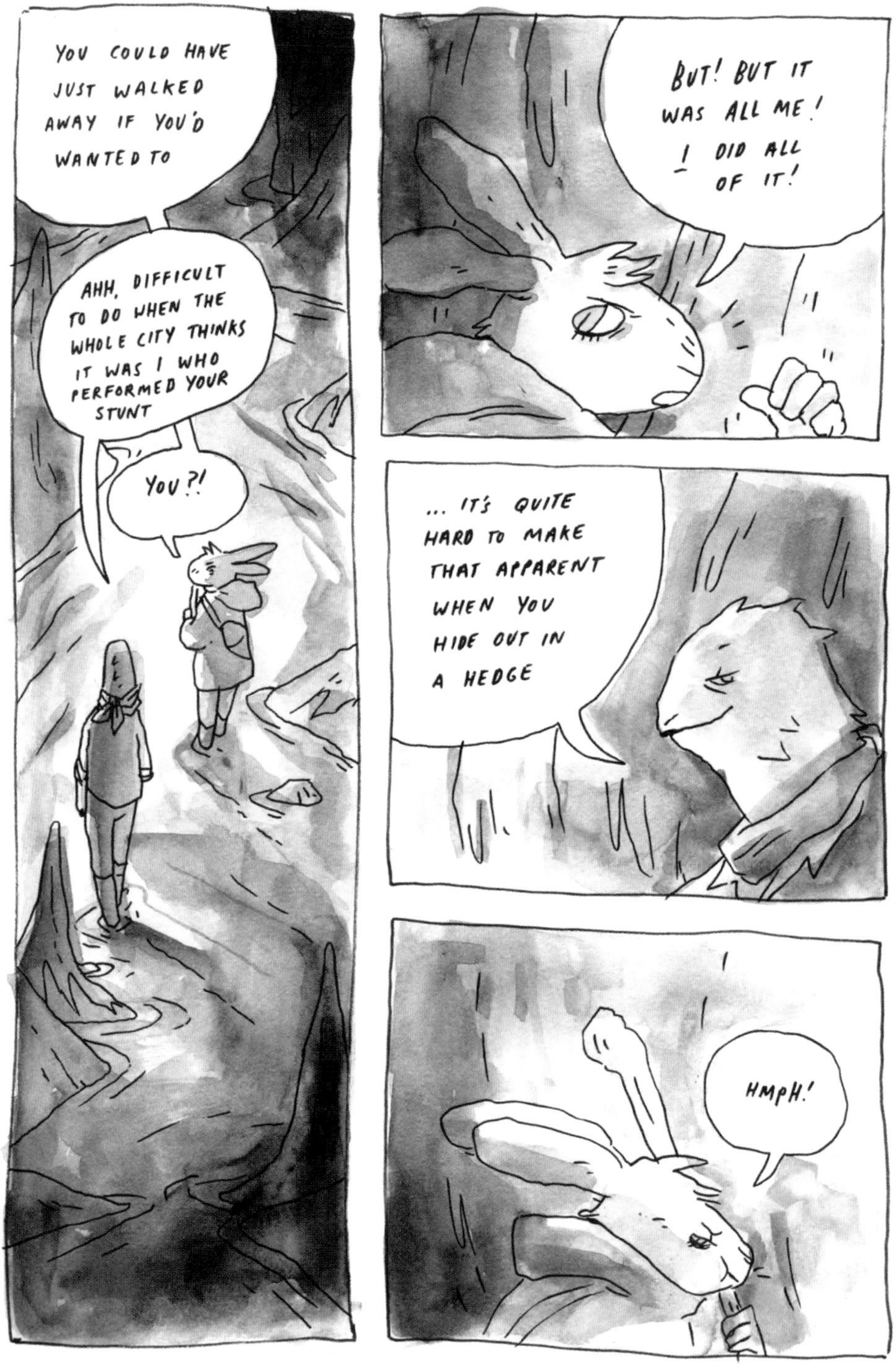
YOU COULD HAVE JUST WALKED AWAY IF YOU'D WANTED TO
AHH, DIFFICULT TO DO WHEN THE WHOLE CITY THINKS IT WAS I WHO PERFORMED YOUR STUNT
YOU?!
BUT! BUT IT WAS ALL ME! I DID ALL OF IT!
... IT'S QUITE HARD TO MAKE THAT APPARENT WHEN YOU HIDE OUT IN A HEDGE
HMPH!

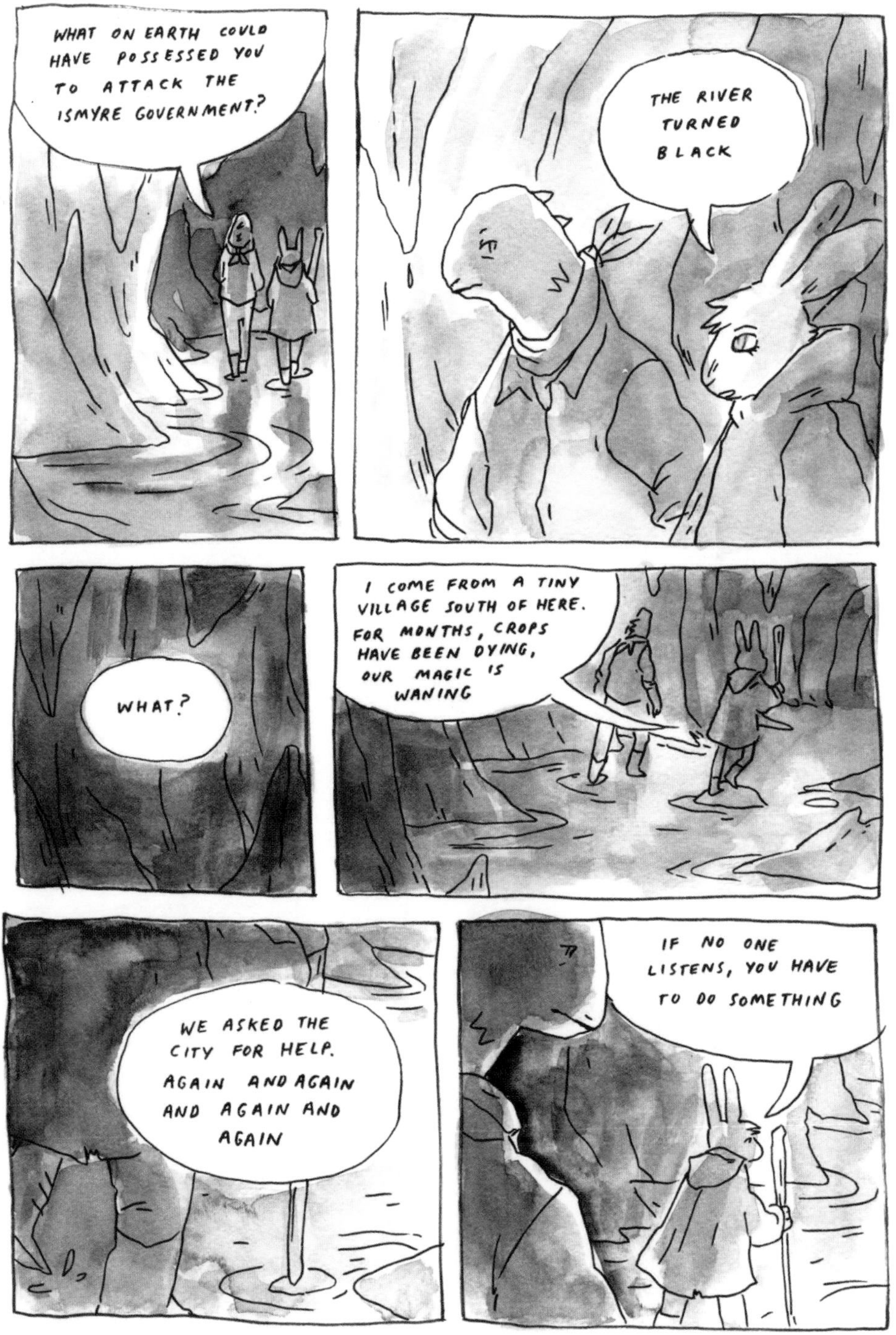
WHAT ON EARTH COULD HAVE POSSESSED YOU TO ATTACK THE ISMYRE GOVERNMENT?
THE RIVER TURNED BLACK
WHAT?
I COME FROM A TINY VILLAGE SOUTH OF HERE. FOR MONTHS, CROPS HAVE BEEN DYING, OUR MAGIC IS WANING
WE ASKED THE CITY FOR HELP. AGAIN AND AGAIN AND AGAIN AND AGAIN
IF NO ONE LISTENS, YOU HAVE TO DO SOMETHING

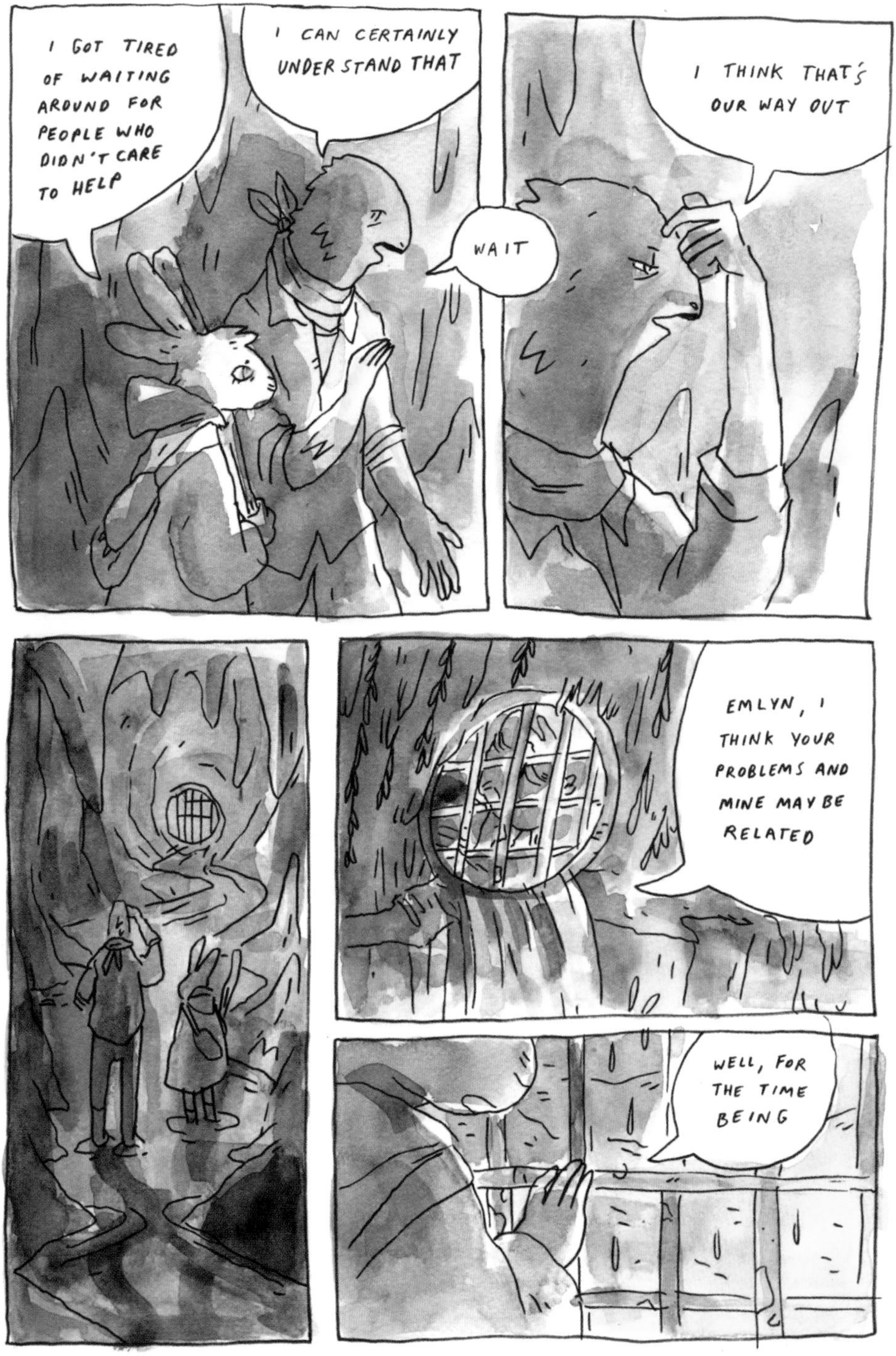
I GOT TIRED OF WAITING AROUND FOR PEOPLE WHO DIDN'T CARE TO HELP
I CAN CERTAINLY UNDERSTAND THAT
WAIT
I THINK THAT'S OUR WAY OUT
EMLYN, I THINK YOUR PROBLEMS AND MINE MAY BE RELATED
WELL, FOR THE TIME BEING

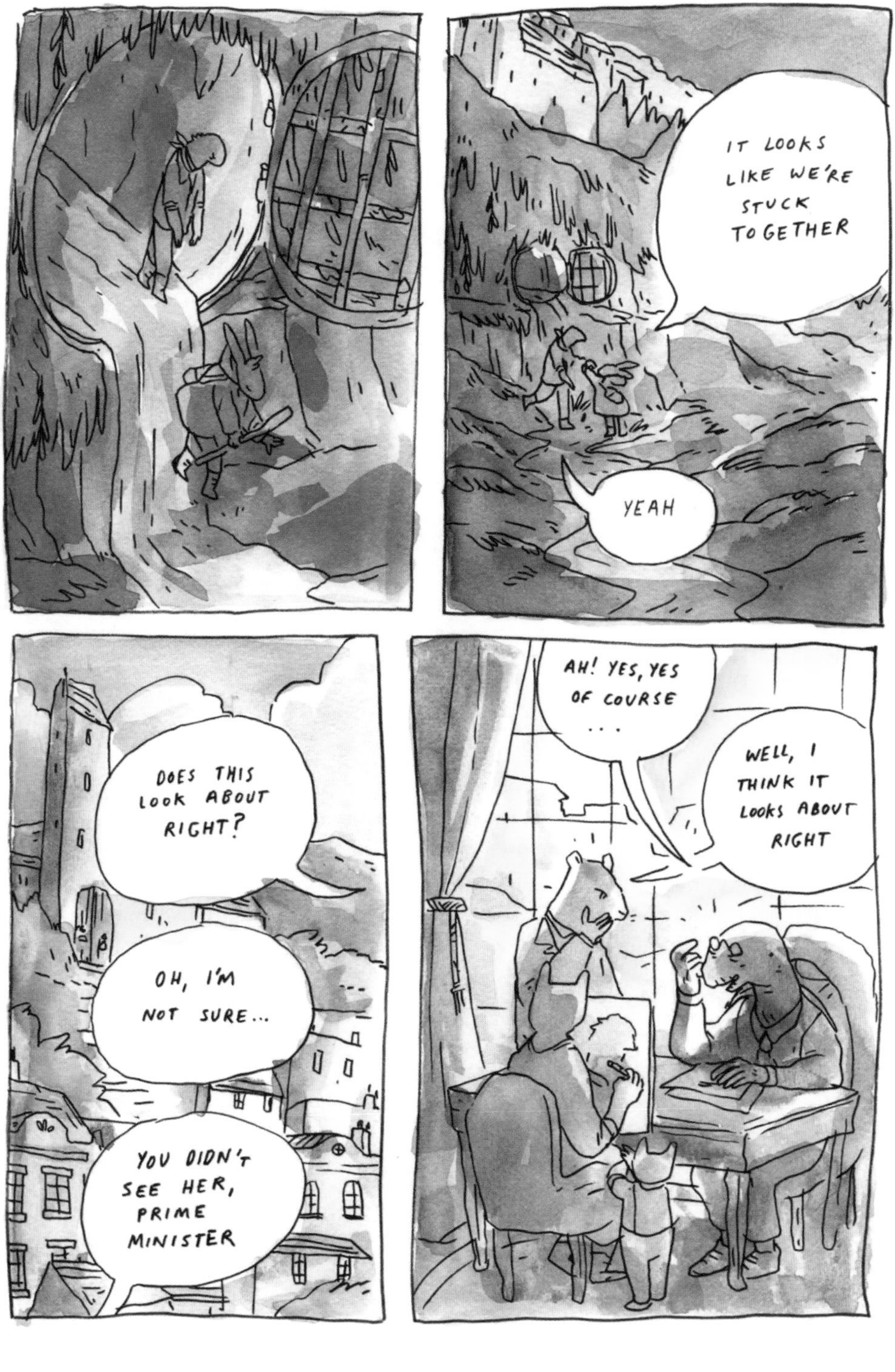
IT LOOKS LIKE WE'RE STUCK TOGETHER
YEAH
DOES THIS LOOK ABOUT RIGHT?
OH, I'M NOT SURE...
YOU DIDN'T SEE HER, PRIME MINISTER
AH! YES, YES OF COURSE . . .
WELL, I THINK IT LOOKS ABOUT RIGHT

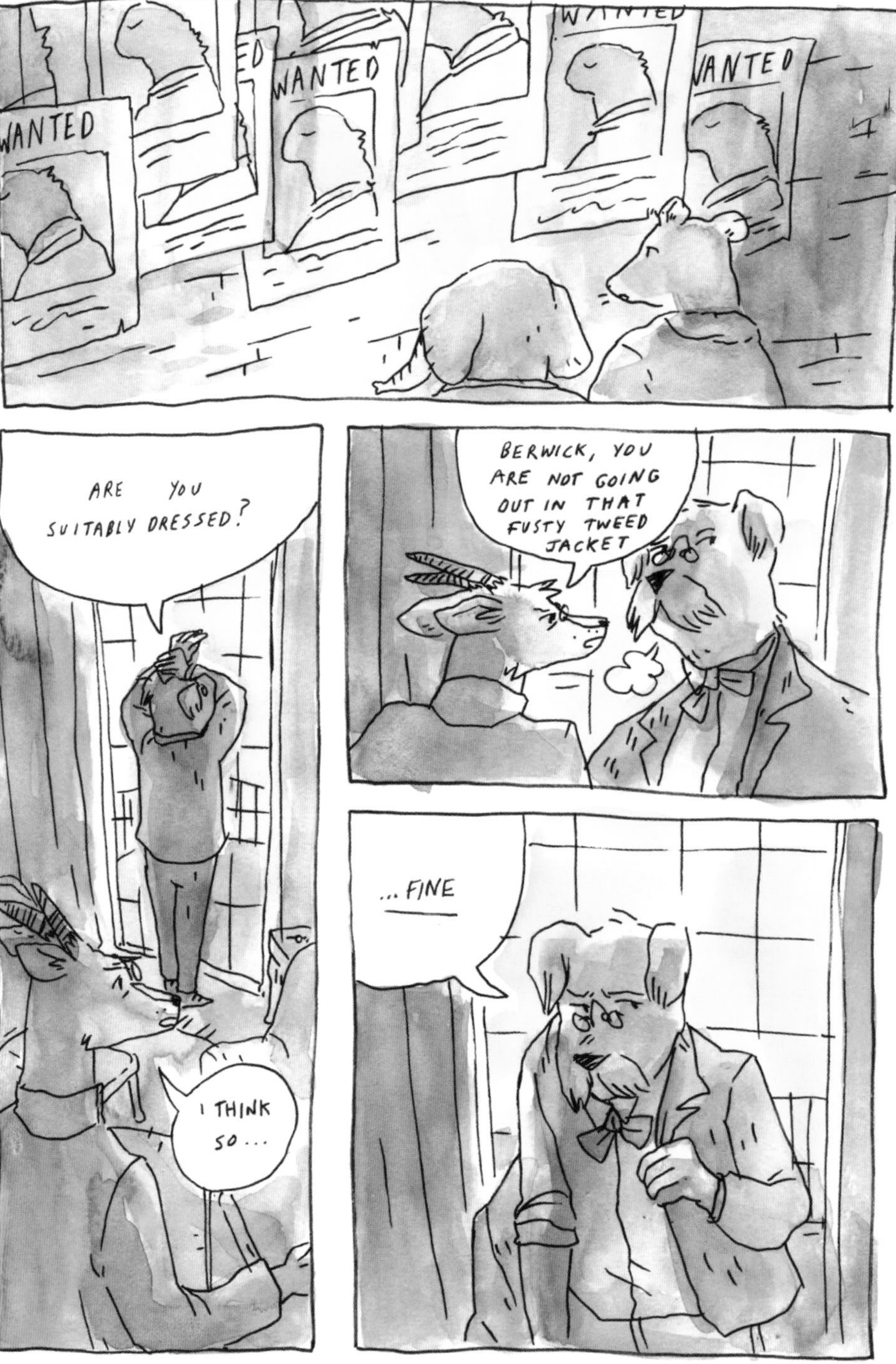
WANTED
WANTED
WANTED
WANTED
ARE YOU SUITABLY DRESSED?
I THINK SO...
BERWICK, YOU ARE NOT GOING OUT IN THAT FUSTY TWEED JACKET
...FINE

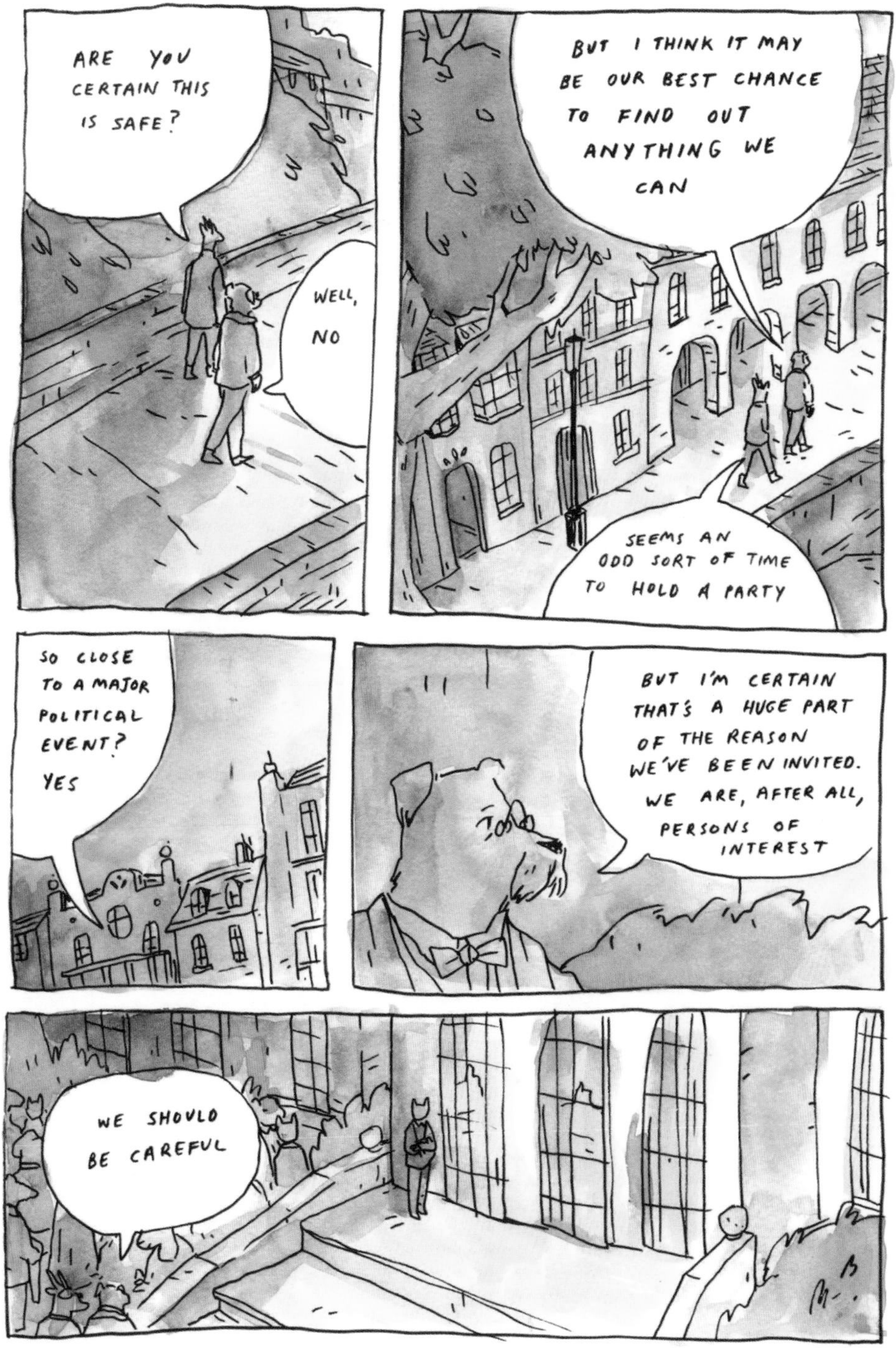
ARE YOU CERTAIN THIS IS SAFE?
WELL, NO
BUT I THINK IT MAY BE OUR BEST CHANCE TO FIND OUT ANYTHING WE CAN
SEEMS AN ODD SORT OF TIME TO HOLD A PARTY
SO CLOSE TO A MAJOR POLITICAL EVENT? YES
BUT I'M CERTAIN THAT'S A HUGE PART OF THE REASON WE'VE BEEN INVITED. WE ARE, AFTER ALL, PERSONS OF INTEREST
WE SHOULD BE CAREFUL

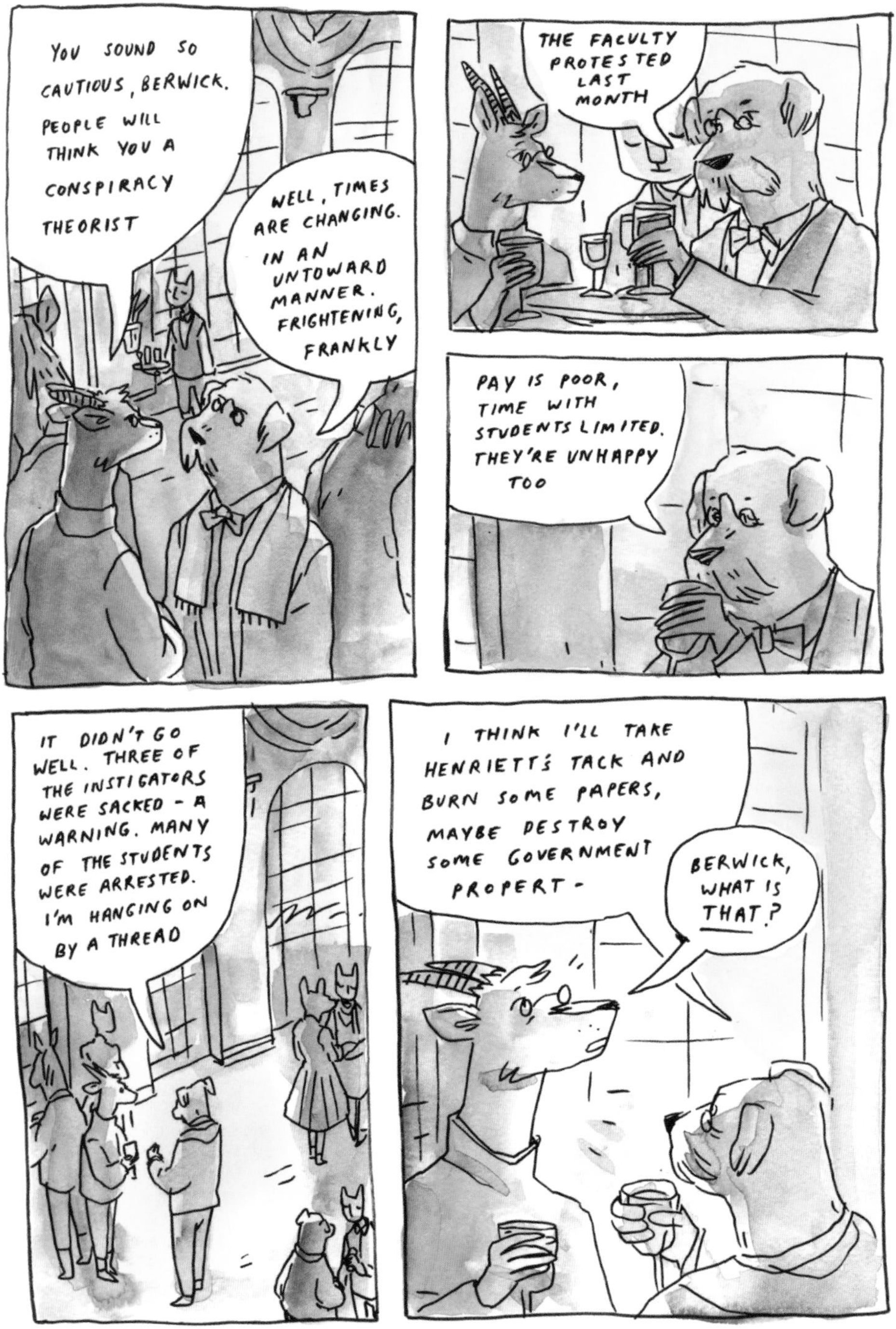
YOU SOUND SO CAUTIOUS, BERWICK. PEOPLE WILL THINK YOU A CONSPIRACY THEORIST
WELL, TIMES ARE CHANGING. IN AN UNTOWARD MANNER. FRIGHTENING, FRANKLY
THE FACULTY PROTESTED LAST MONTH
PAY IS POOR, TIME WITH STUDENTS LIMITED. THEY'RE UNHAPPY TOO
IT DIDN'T GO WELL. THREE OF THE INSTIGATORS WERE SACKED - A WARNING. MANY OF THE STUDENTS WERE ARRESTED. I'M HANGING ON BY A THREAD
I THINK I'LL TAKE HENRIETT'S TACK AND BURN SOME PAPERS, MAYBE DESTROY SOME GOVERNMENT PROPERT -
BERWICK, WHAT IS THAT?

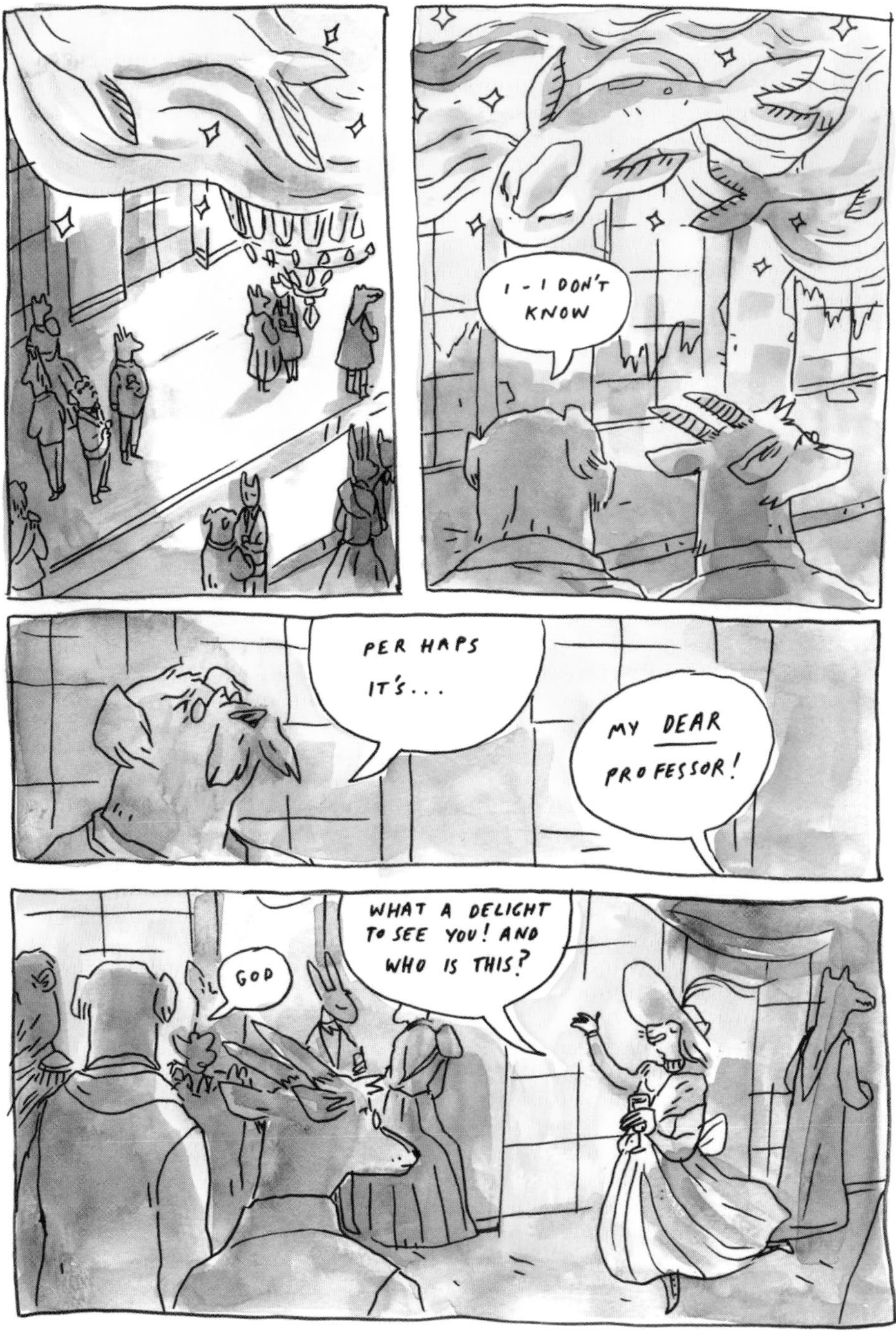
I-I DON'T KNOW
PERHAPS IT'S...
MY DEAR PROFESSOR!
GOD
WHAT A DELIGHT TO SEE YOU! AND WHO IS THIS?

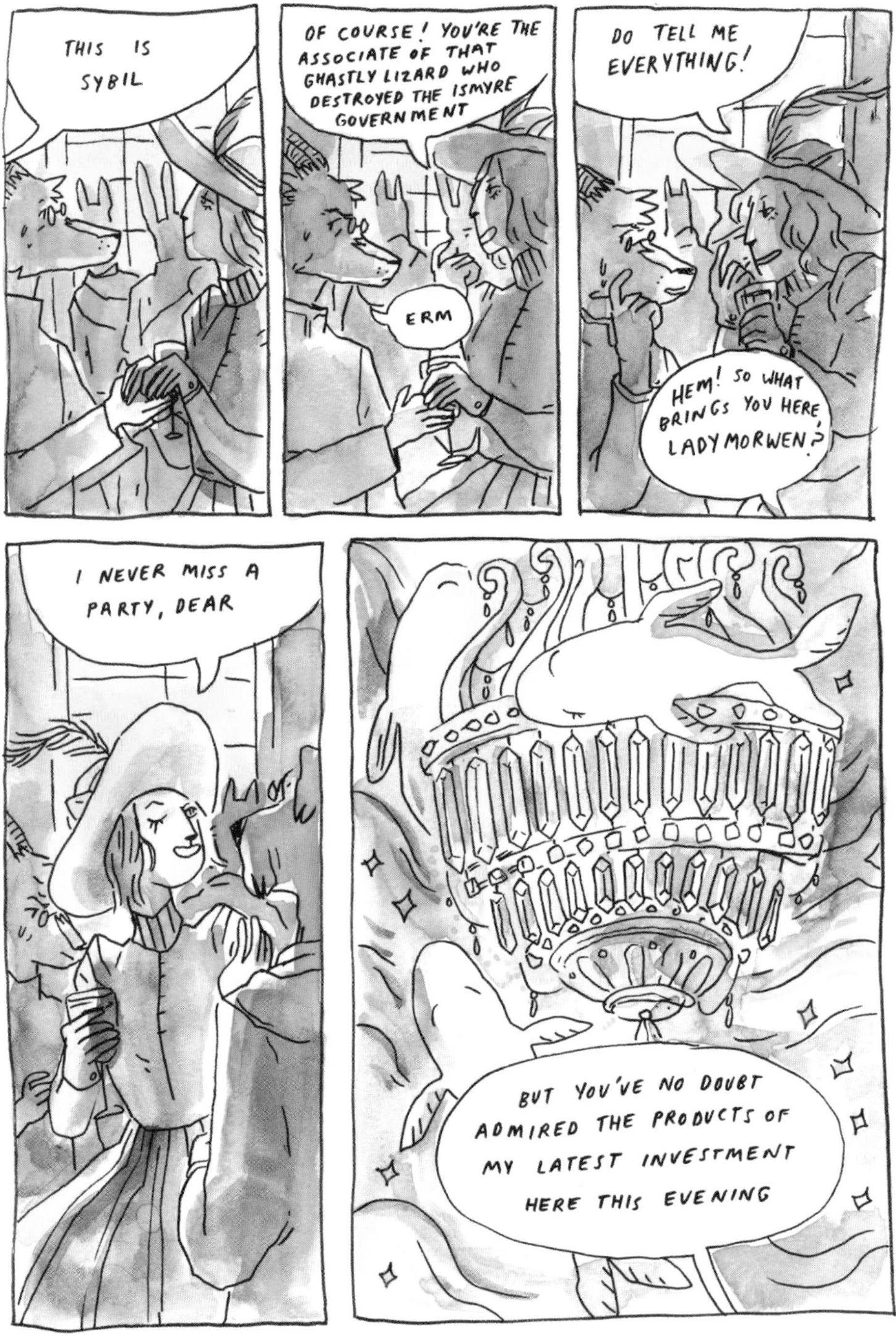
THIS IS SYBIL
OF COURSE! YOU'RE THE ASSOCIATE OF THAT GHASTLY LIZARD WHO DESTROYED THE ISMYRE GOVERNMENT
ERM
DO TELL ME EVERYTHING!
HEM! SO WHAT BRINGS YOU HERE, LADY MORWEN?
I NEVER MISS A PARTY, DEAR
BUT YOU'VE NO DOUBT ADMIRED THE PRODUCTS OF MY LATEST INVESTMENT HERE THIS EVENING

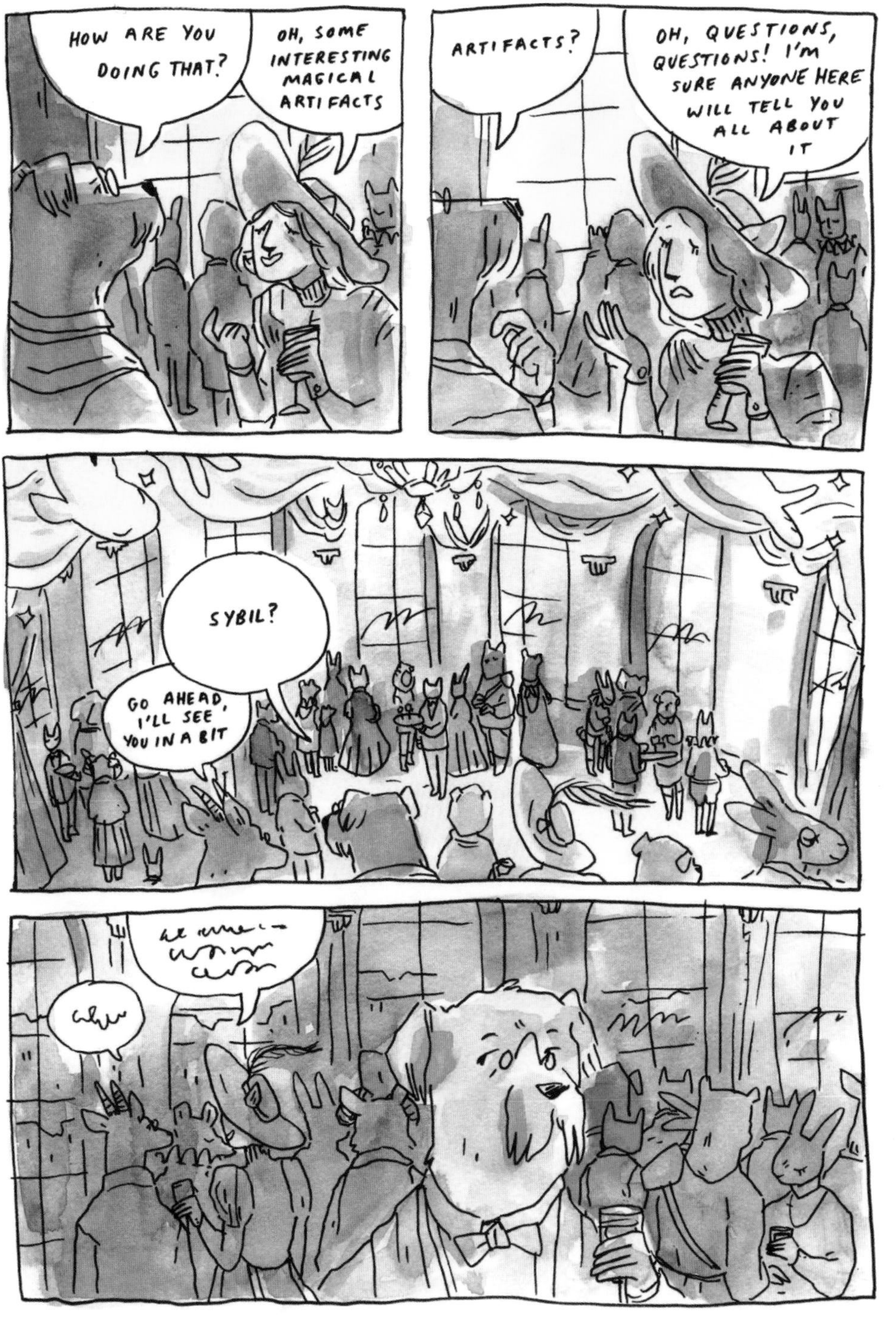
HOW ARE YOU DOING THAT?
OH, SOME INTERESTING MAGICAL ARTIFACTS
ARTIFACTS?
OH, QUESTIONS, QUESTIONS! I'M SURE ANYONE HERE WILL TELL YOU ALL ABOUT IT
SYBIL?
GO AHEAD, I'LL SEE YOU IN A BIT

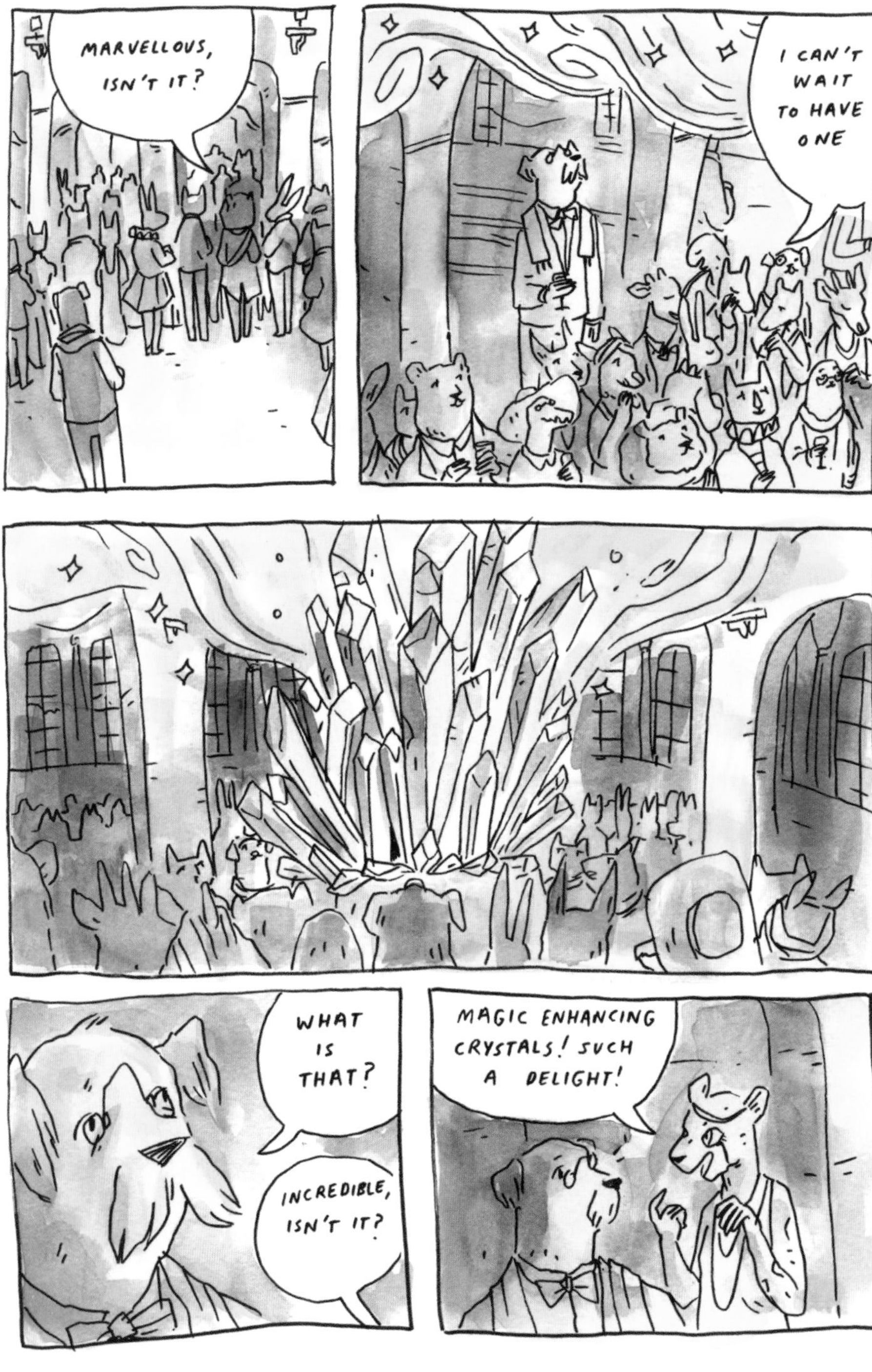
MARVELLOUS, ISN'T IT?
I CAN'T WAIT TO HAVE ONE
WHAT IS THAT?
INCREDIBLE, ISN'T IT?
MAGIC ENHANCING CRYSTALS! SUCH A DELIGHT!

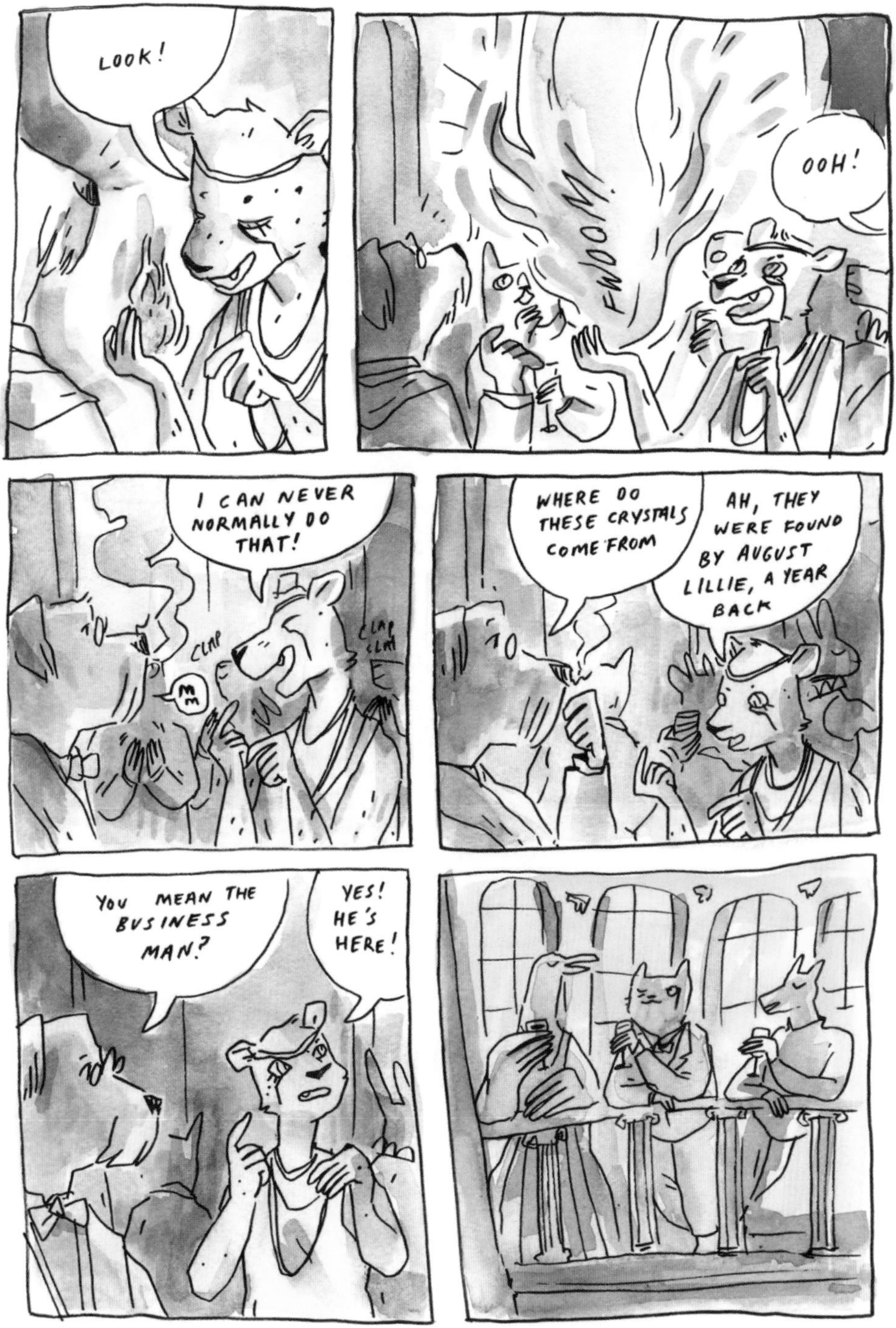
LOOK!
FWOOM!
OOH!
I CAN NEVER NORMALLY DO THAT!
CLAP
CLAP CLAP
MM
WHERE DO THESE CRYSTALS COME FROM
AH, THEY WERE FOUND BY AUGUST LILLIE, A YEAR BACK
YOU MEAN THE BUSINESS MAN?
YES! HE'S HERE!

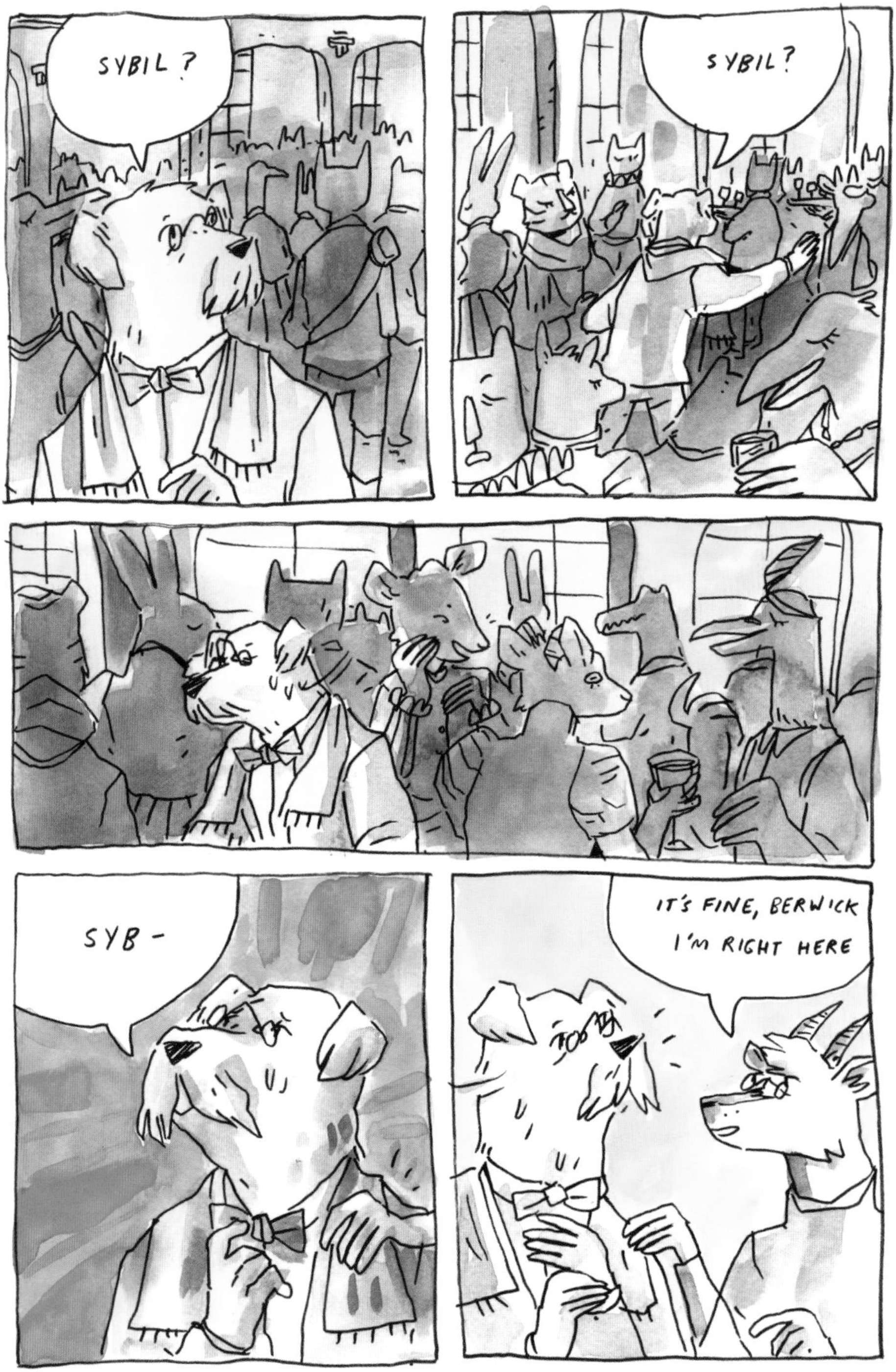
SYBIL ?
SYBIL?
SYB -
IT'S FINE, BERWICK
I'M RIGHT HERE

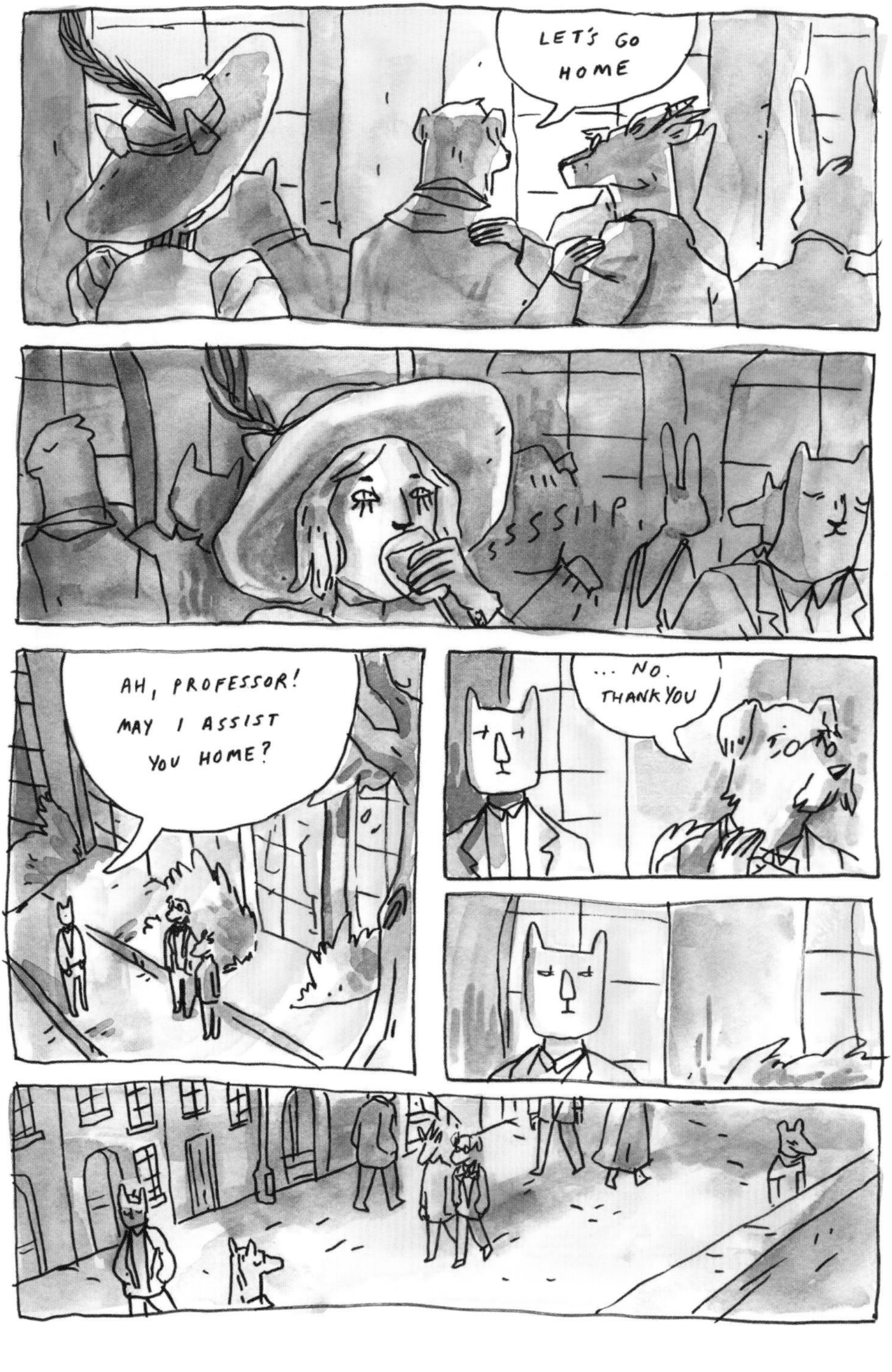
LET'S GO HOME
SSSSIIP.
AH, PROFESSOR! MAY I ASSIST YOU HOME?
... NO. THANK YOU

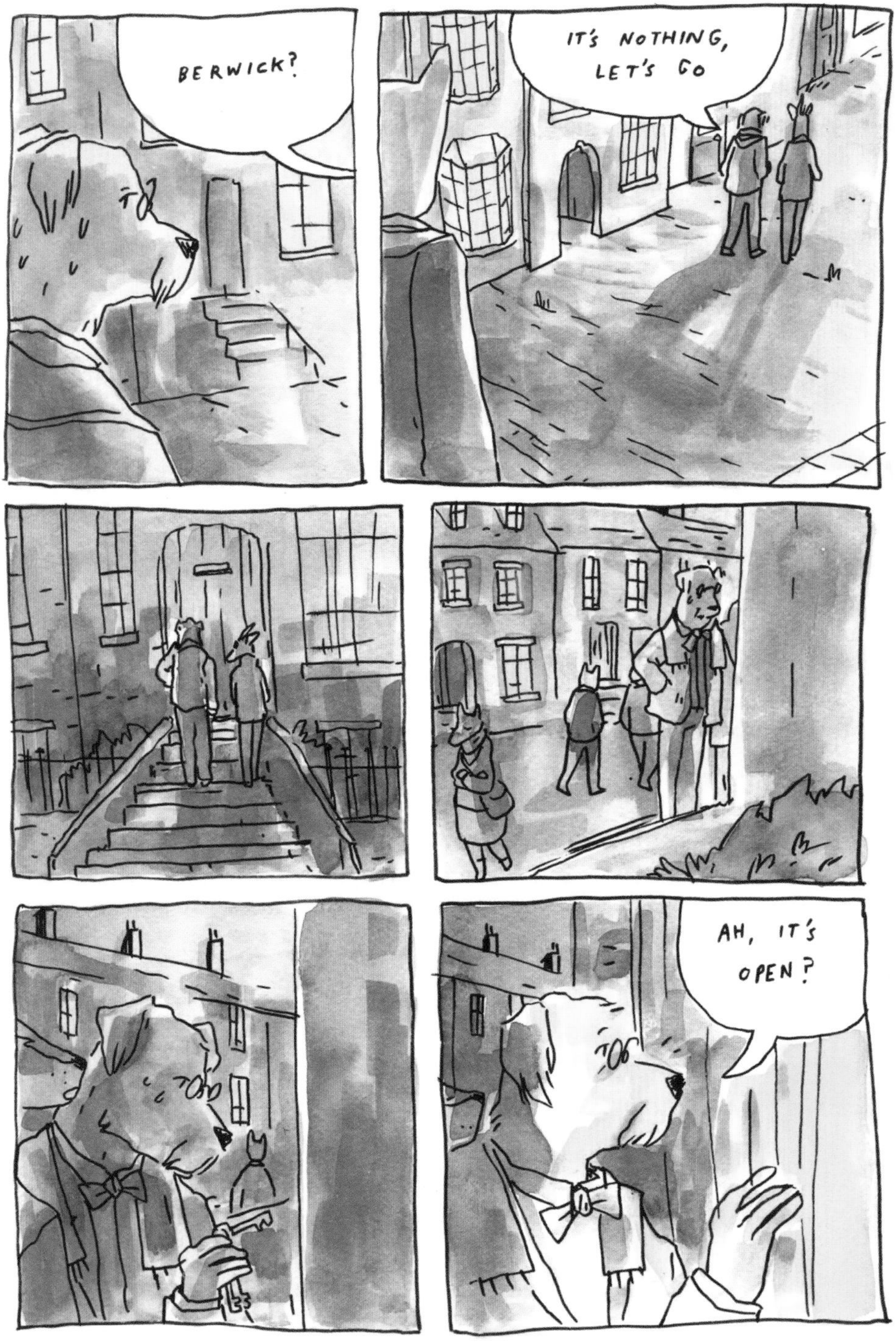

BERWICK?
IT'S NOTHING, LET'S GO
AH, IT'S OPEN?

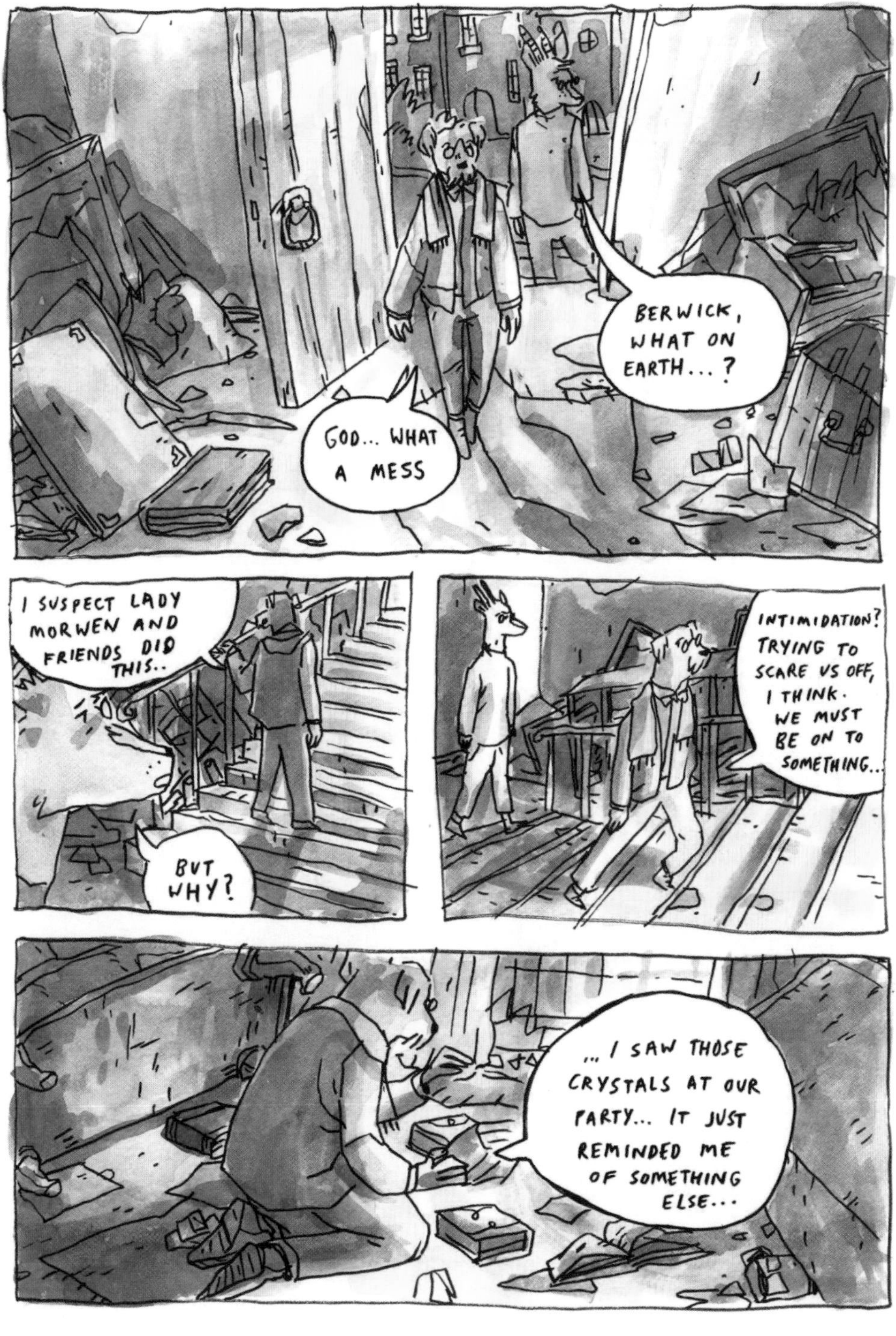

BERWICK, WHAT ON EARTH...?
GOD... WHAT A MESS
I SUSPECT LADY MORWEN AND FRIENDS DID THIS..
BUT WHY?
INTIMIDATION? TRYING TO SCARE US OFF, I THINK. WE MUST BE ON TO SOMETHING...
... I SAW THOSE CRYSTALS AT OUR PARTY... IT JUST REMINDED ME OF SOMETHING ELSE...

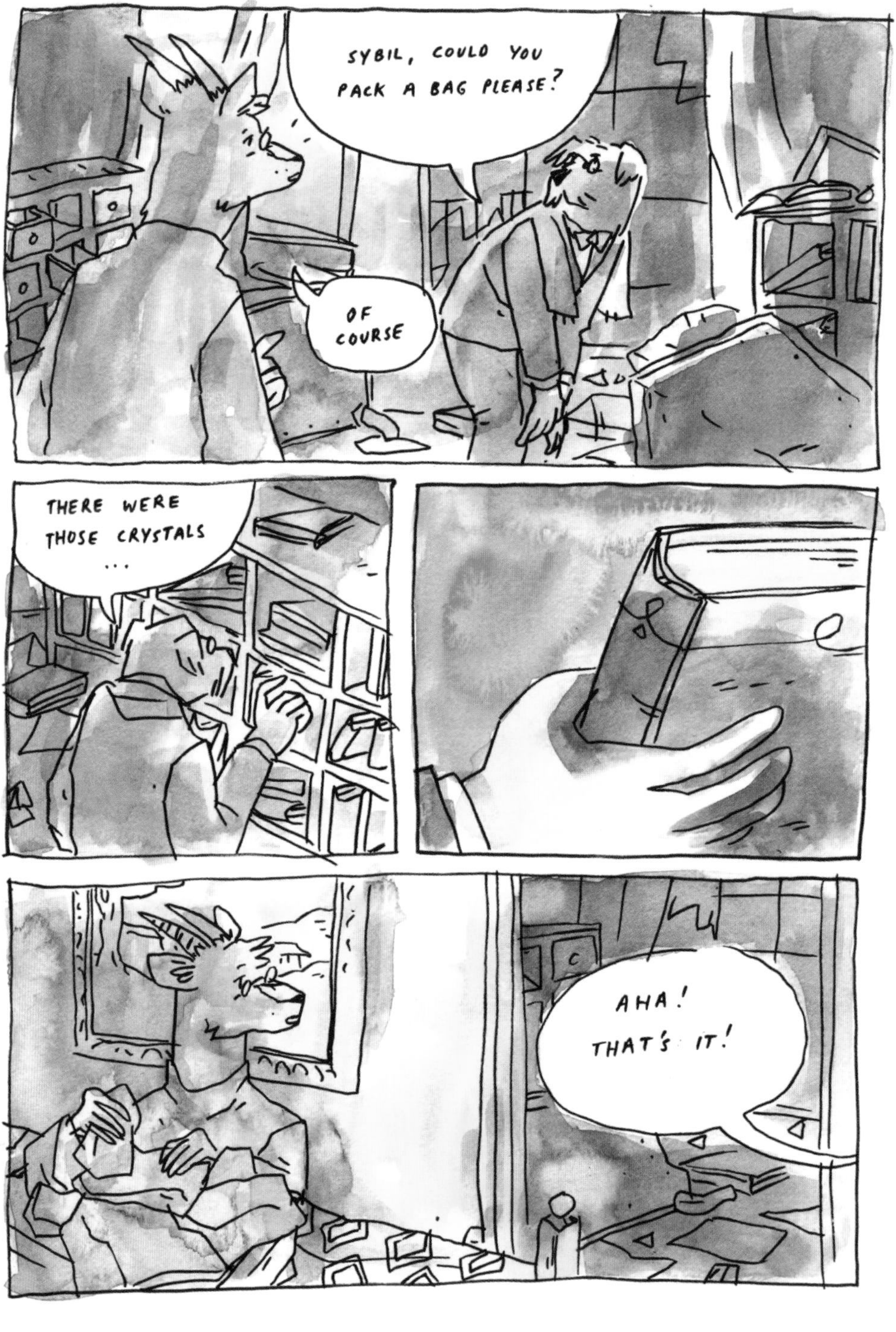
SYBIL, COULD YOU PACK A BAG PLEASE?
OF COURSE
THERE WERE THOSE CRYSTALS ...
AHA! THAT'S IT!

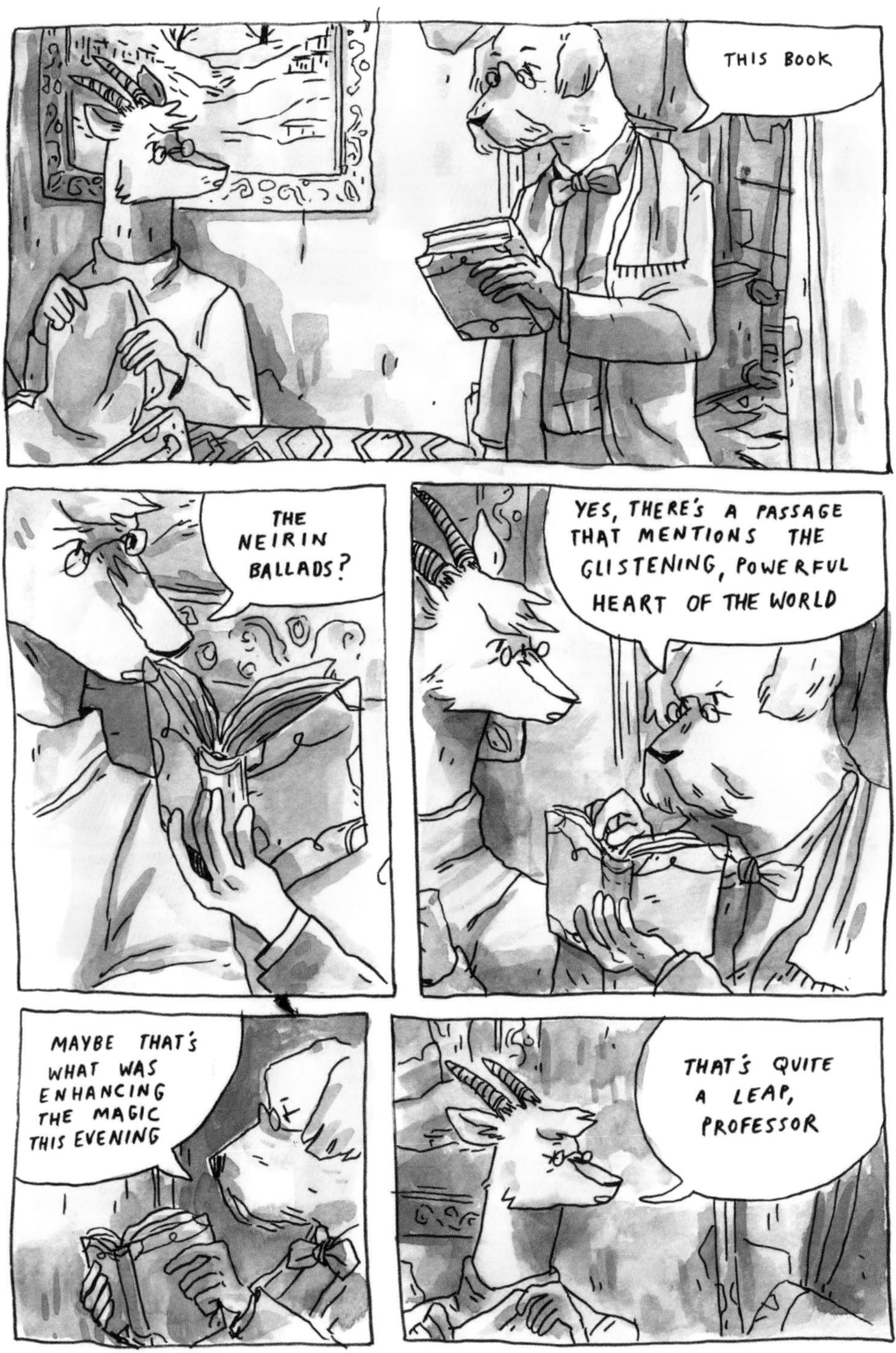
THIS BOOK
THE NEIRIN BALLADS?
YES, THERE'S A PASSAGE THAT MENTIONS THE GLISTENING, POWERFUL HEART OF THE WORLD
MAYBE THAT'S WHAT WAS ENHANCING THE MAGIC THIS EVENING
THAT'S QUITE A LEAP, PROFESSOR

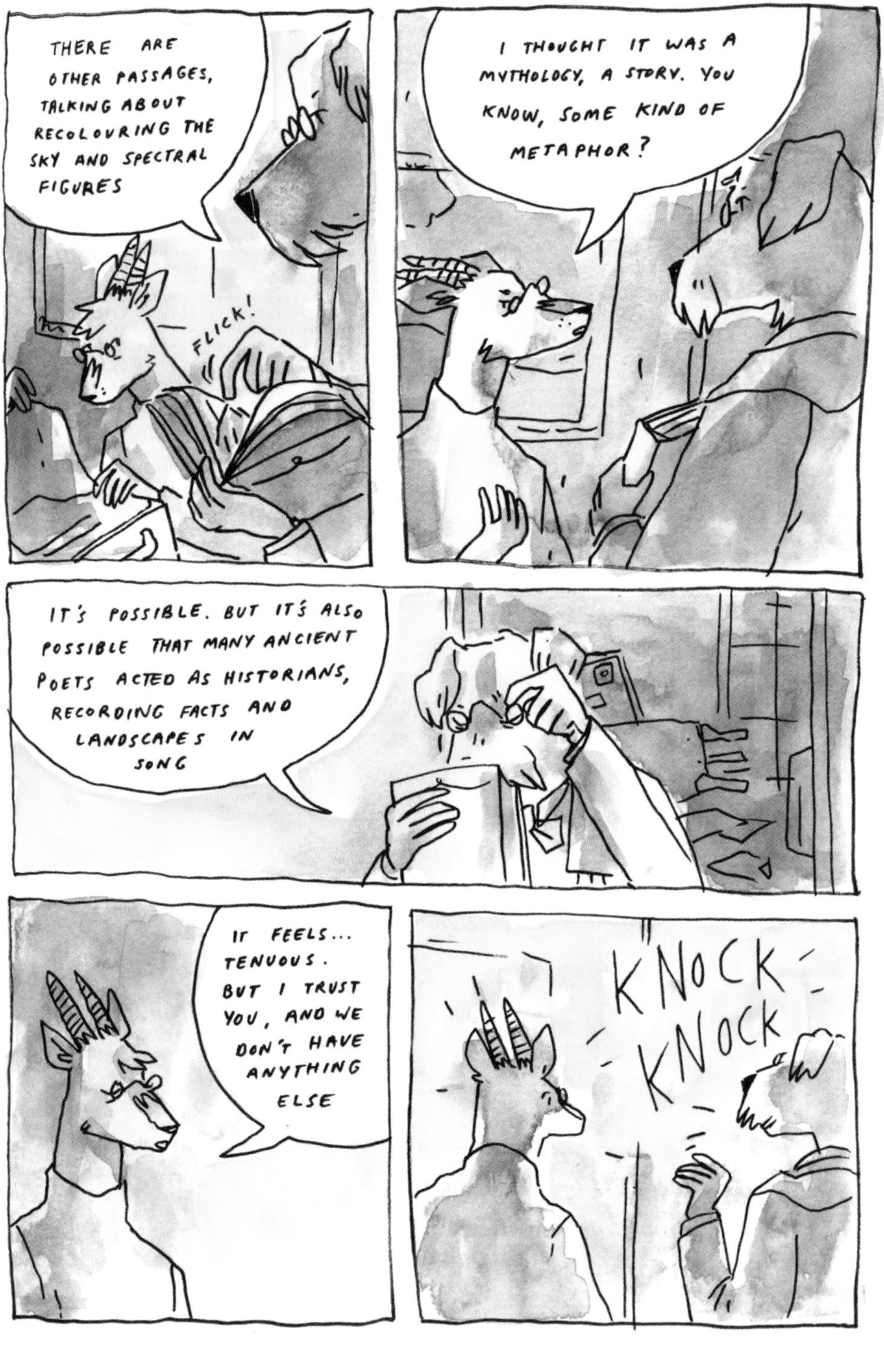
THERE ARE OTHER PASSAGES, TALKING ABOUT RECOLOURING THE SKY AND SPECTRAL FIGURES
FLICK!
I THOUGHT IT WAS A MYTHOLOGY, A STORY. YOU KNOW, SOME KIND OF METAPHOR?
IT'S POSSIBLE. BUT IT'S ALSO POSSIBLE THAT MANY ANCIENT POETS ACTED AS HISTORIANS, RECORDING FACTS AND LANDSCAPES IN SONG
IT FEELS... TENUOUS. BUT I TRUST YOU, AND WE DON'T HAVE ANYTHING ELSE
KNOCK KNOCK

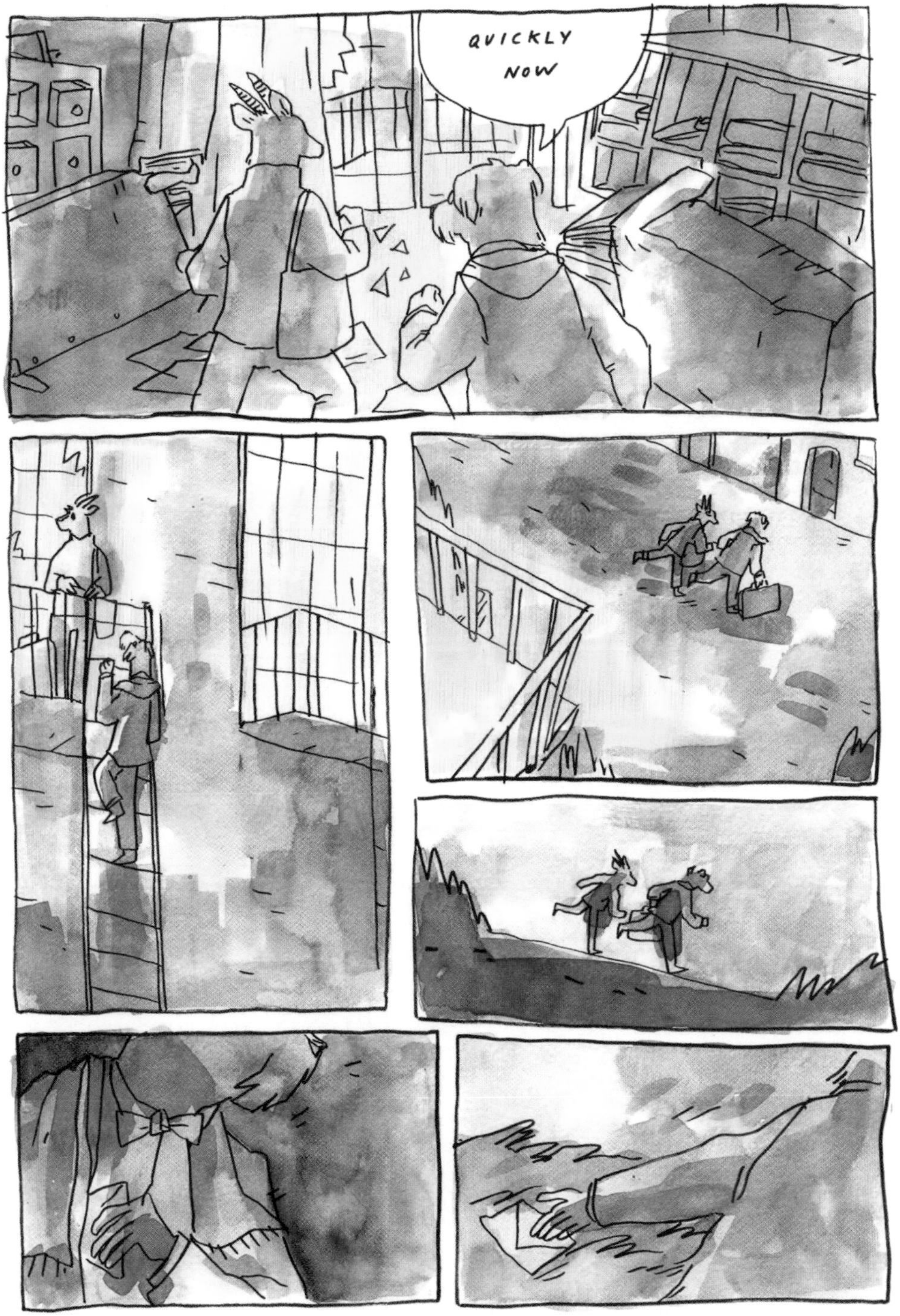
QUICKLY NOW

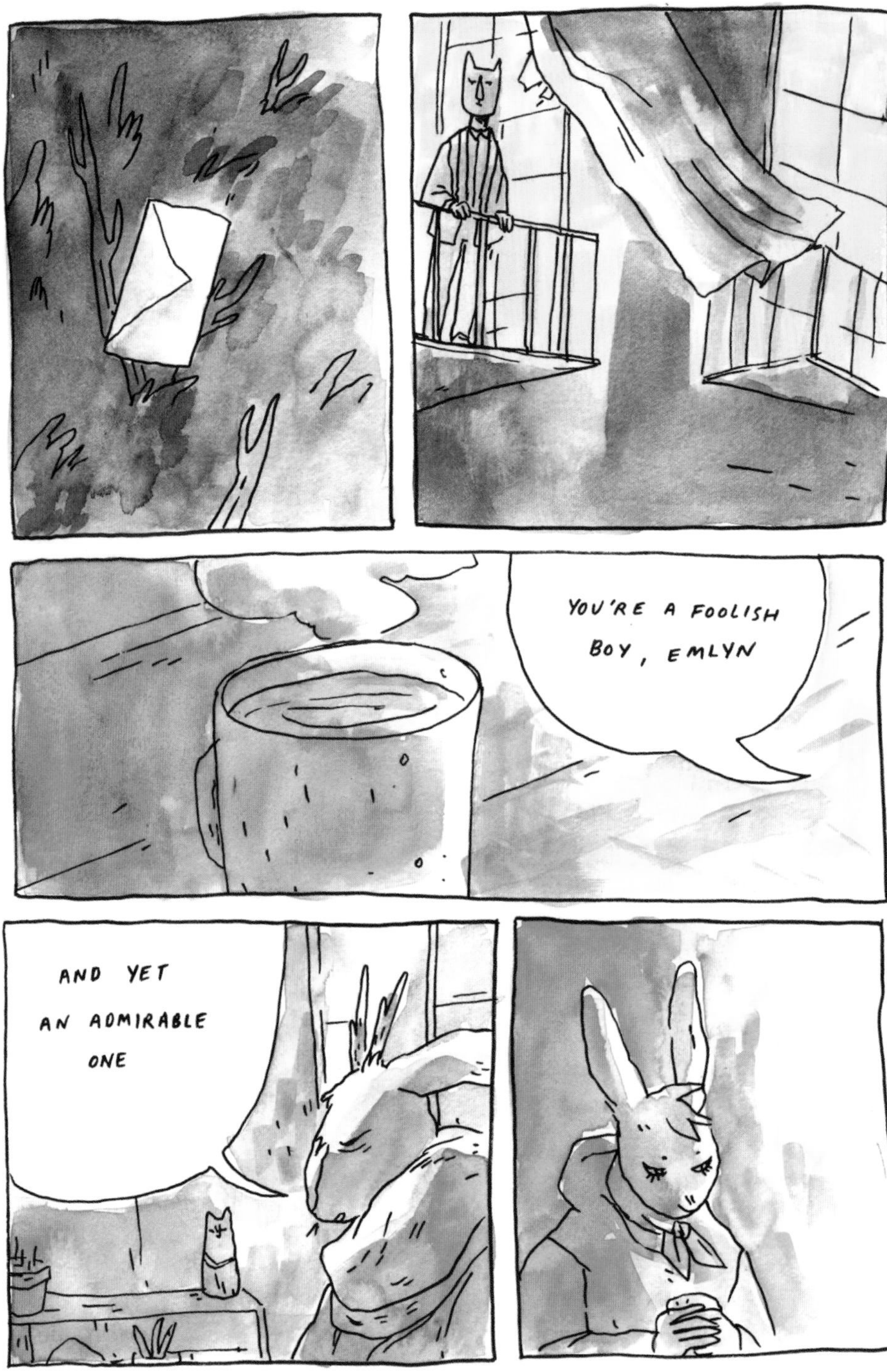
YOU'RE A FOOLISH BOY, EMLYN
AND YET AN ADMIRABLE ONE

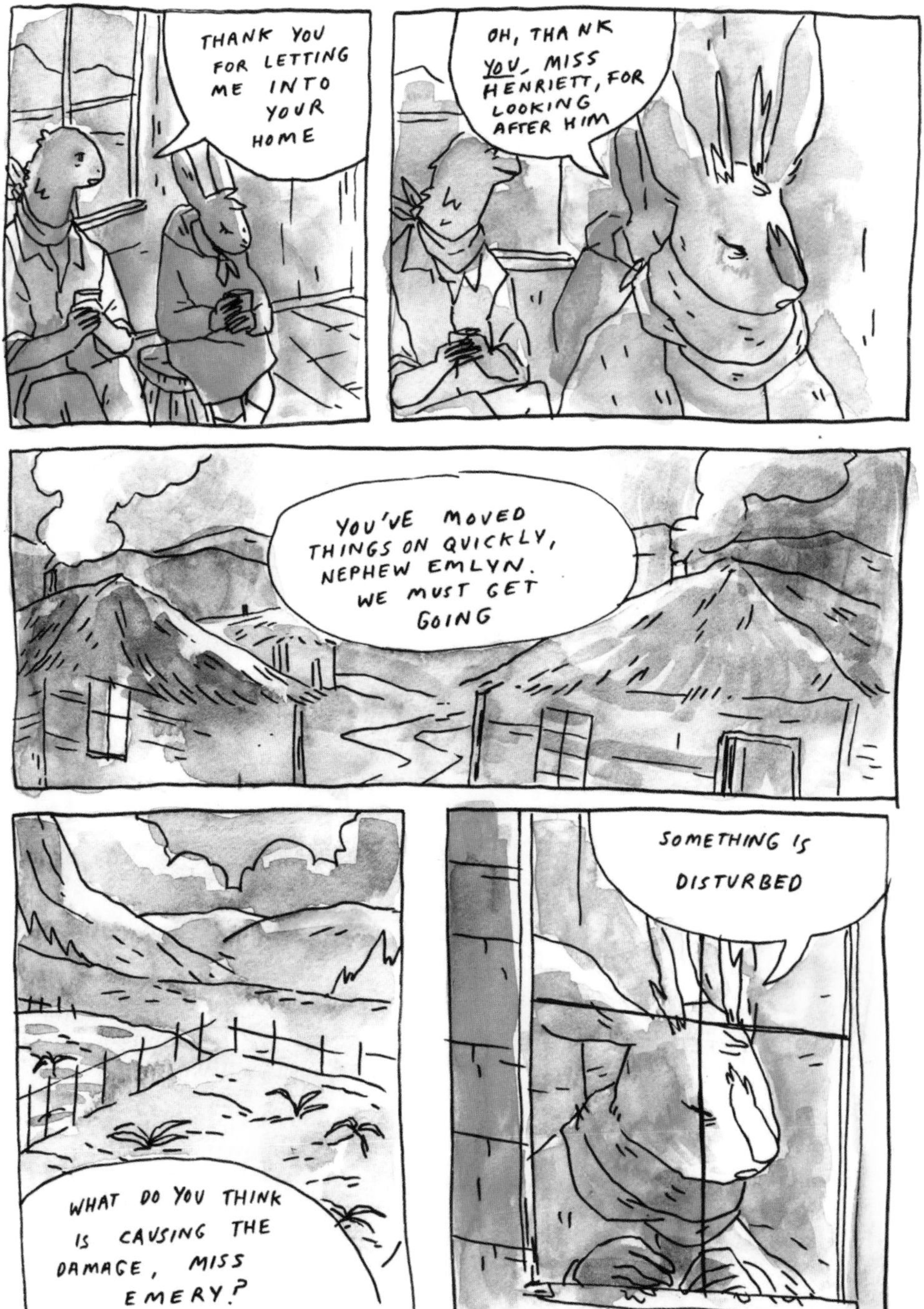
THANK YOU FOR LETTING ME INTO YOUR HOME
OH, THANK YOU, MISS HENRIETT, FOR LOOKING AFTER HIM
YOU'VE MOVED THINGS ON QUICKLY, NEPHEW EMLYN. WE MUST GET GOING
WHAT DO YOU THINK IS CAUSING THE DAMAGE, MISS EMERY?
SOMETHING IS DISTURBED

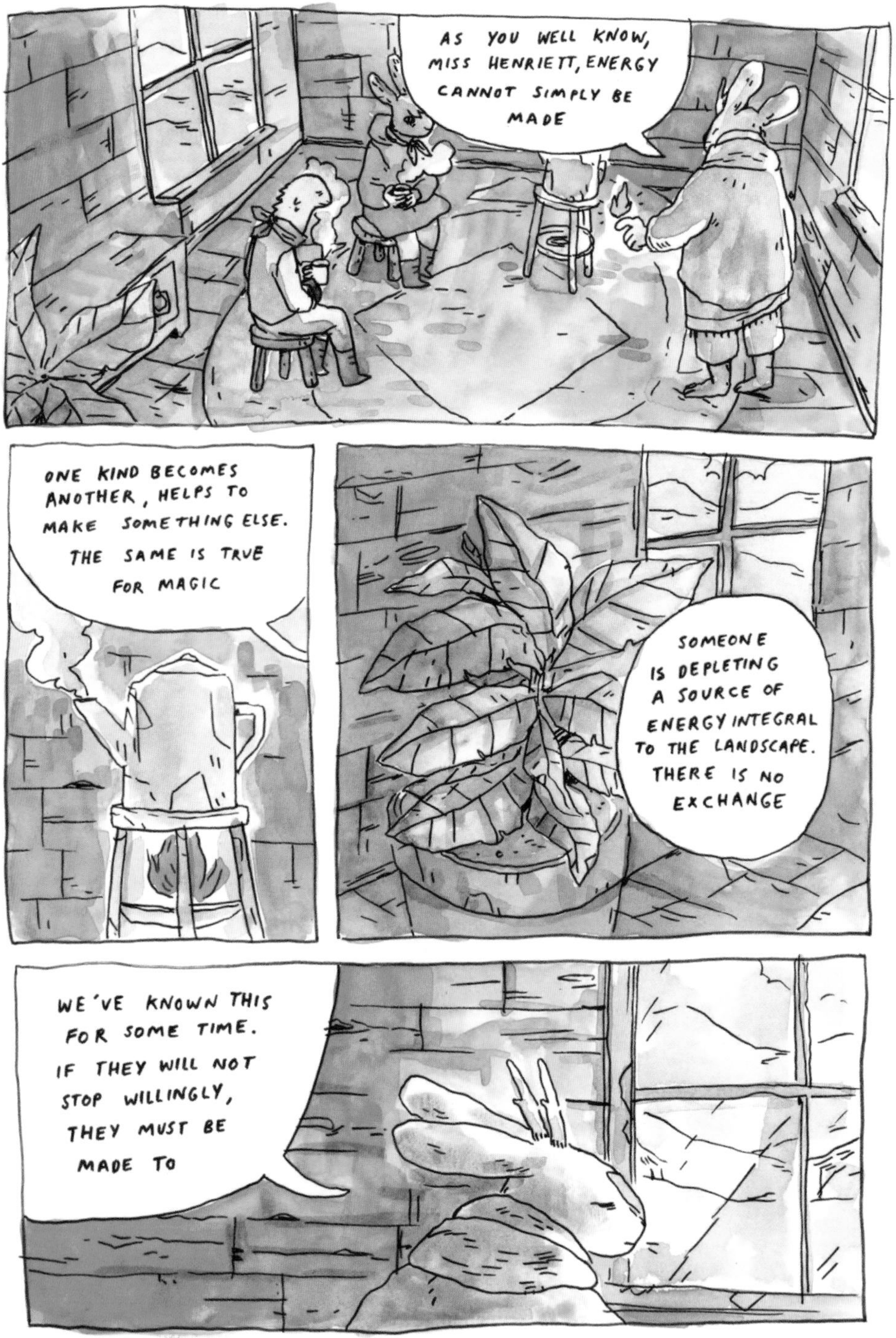
AS YOU WELL KNOW, MISS HENRIETT, ENERGY CANNOT SIMPLY BE MADE
ONE KIND BECOMES ANOTHER, HELPS TO MAKE SOMETHING ELSE. THE SAME IS TRUE FOR MAGIC
SOMEONE IS DEPLETING A SOURCE OF ENERGY INTEGRAL TO THE LANDSCAPE. THERE IS NO EXCHANGE
WE'VE KNOWN THIS FOR SOME TIME. IF THEY WILL NOT STOP WILLINGLY, THEY MUST BE MADE TO

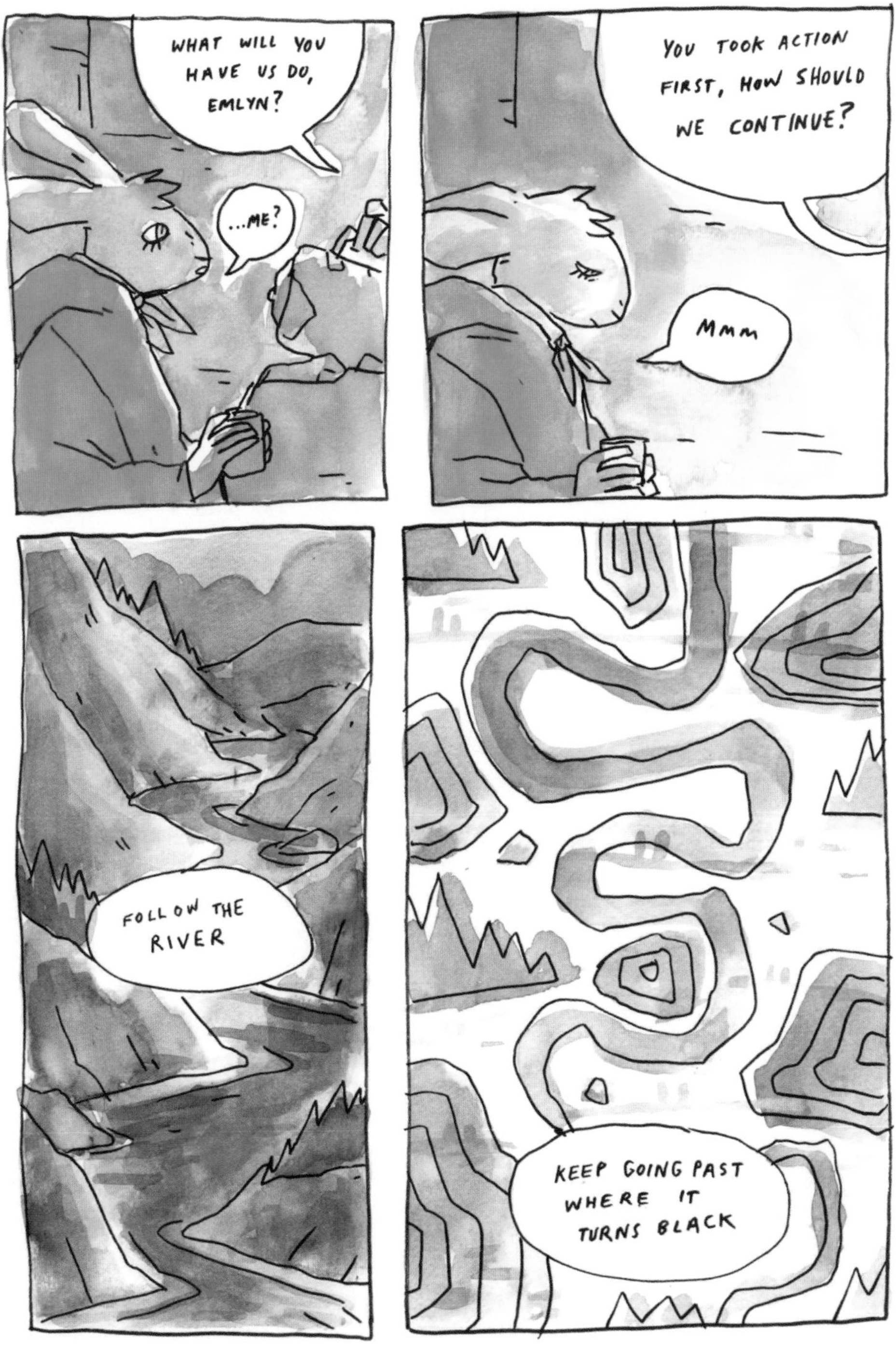
WHAT WILL YOU HAVE US DO, EMLYN?
...ME?
YOU TOOK ACTION FIRST, HOW SHOULD WE CONTINUE?
MMM
FOLLOW THE RIVER
KEEP GOING PAST WHERE IT TURNS BLACK

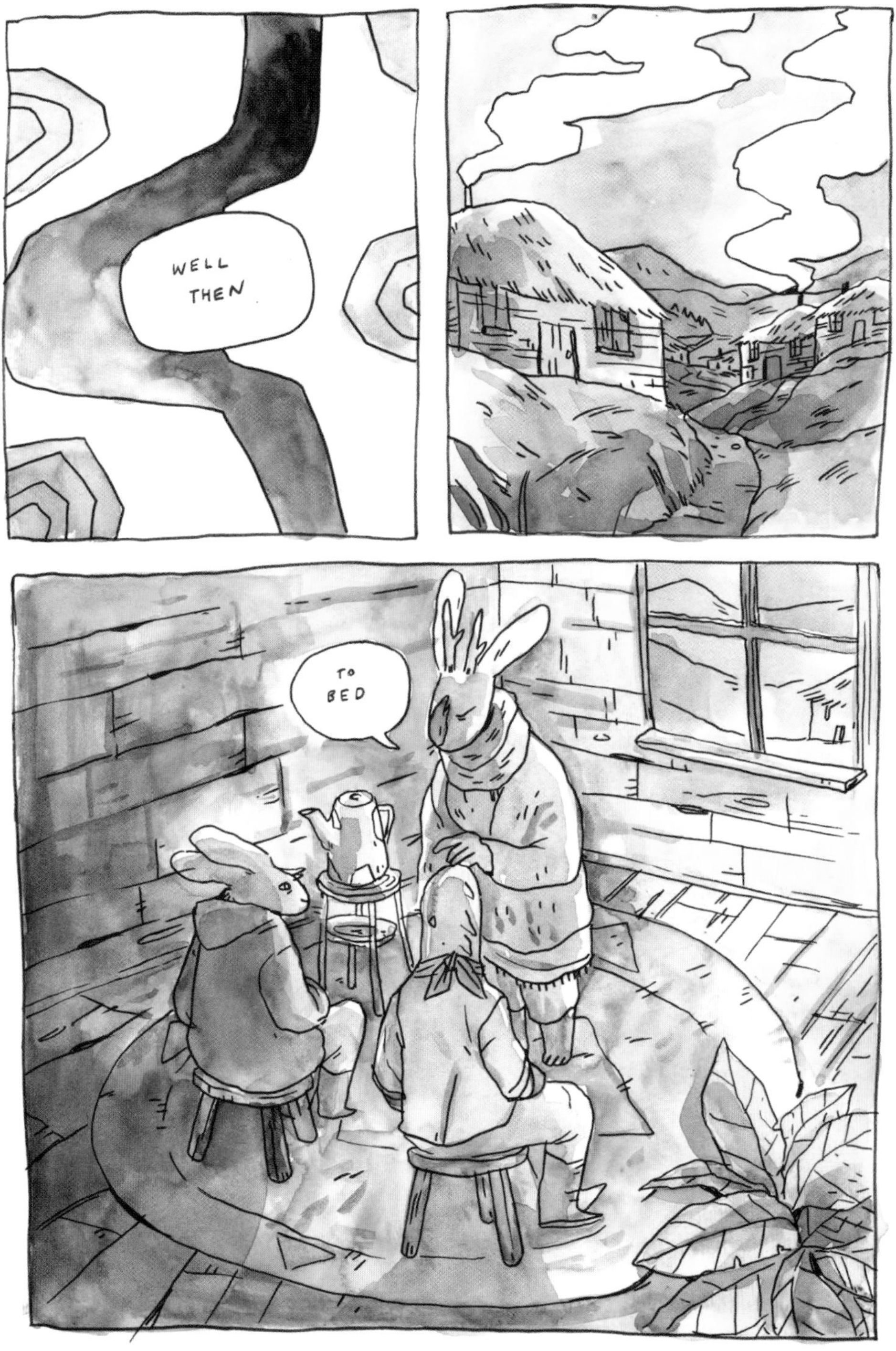
WELL THEN
TO BED

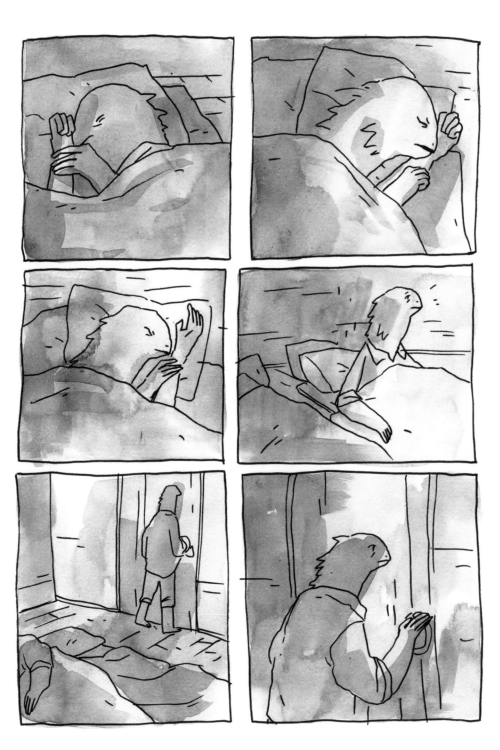

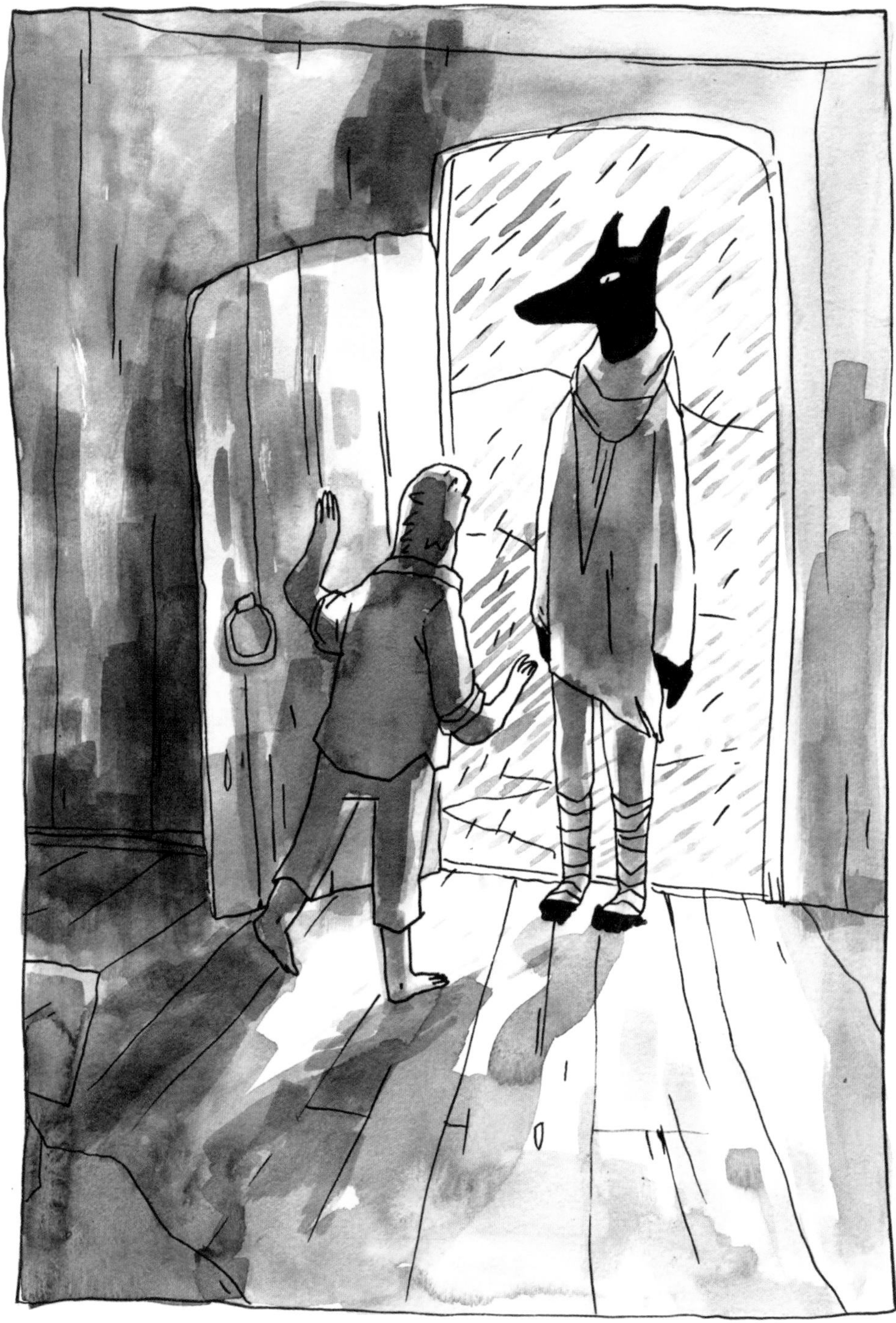

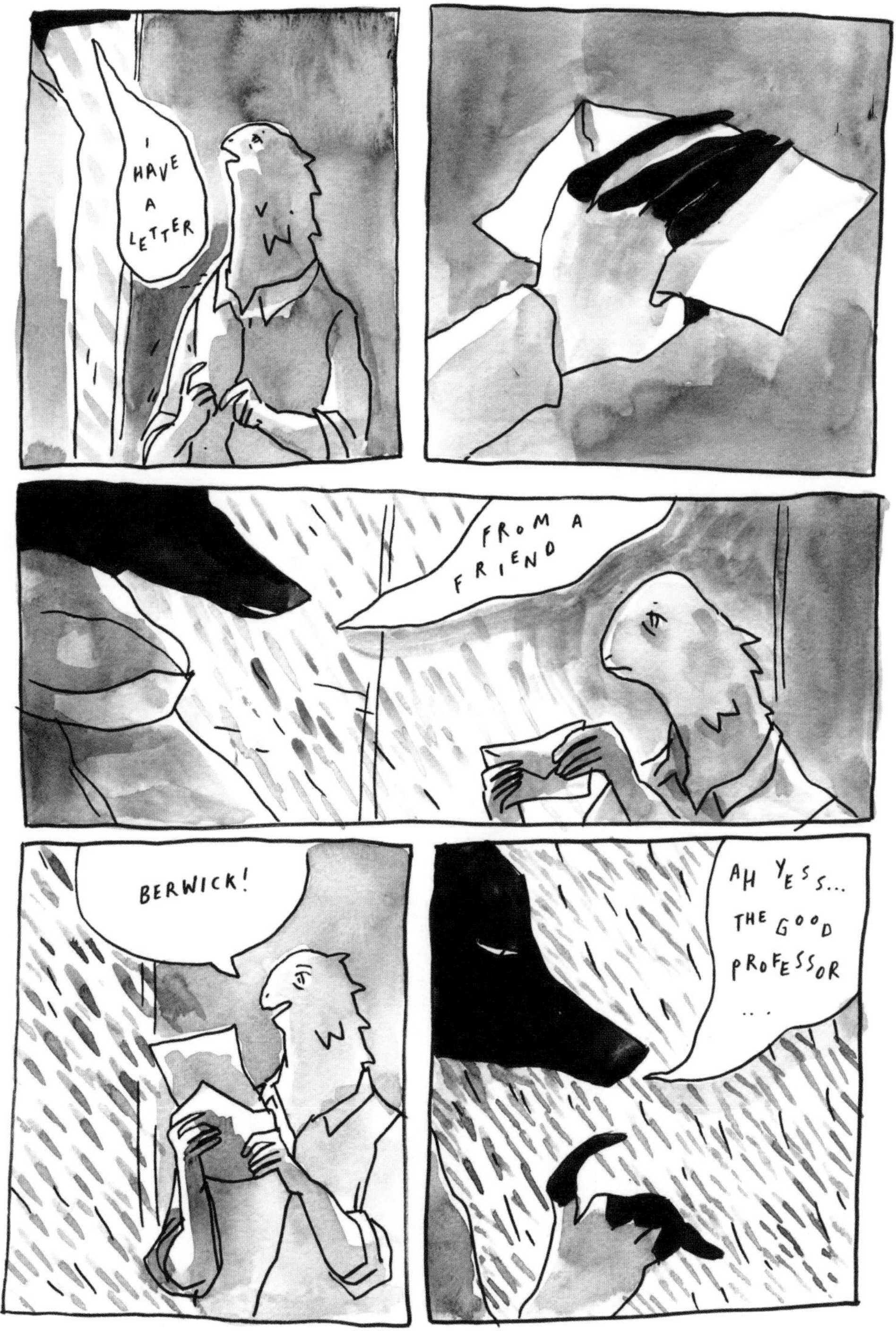
I HAVE A LETTER
FROM A FRIEND
BERWICK!
AH YESS...
THE GOOD PROFESSOR
...

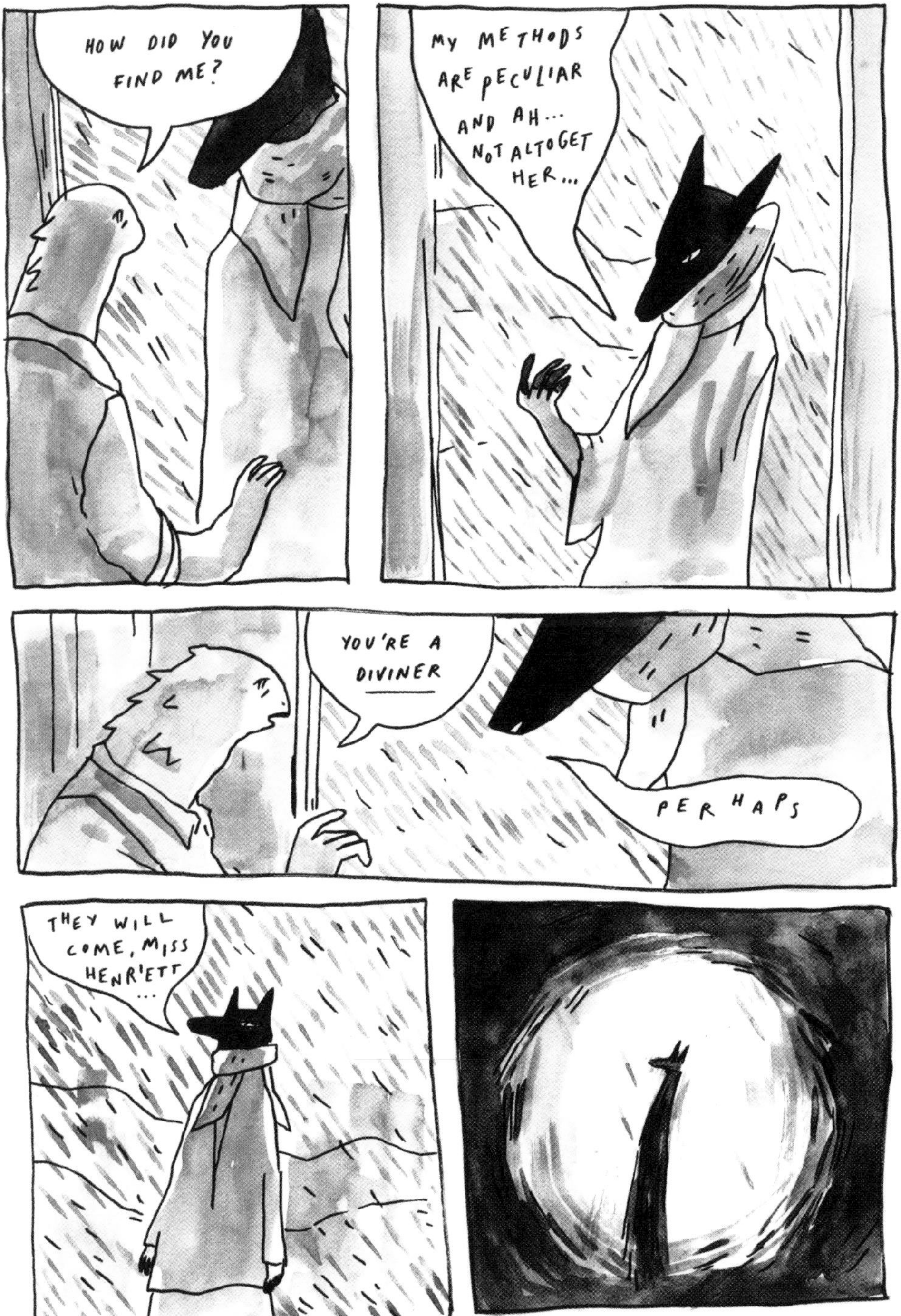
HOW DID YOU FIND ME?
MY METHODS ARE PECULIAR AND AH... NOT ALTOGETHER...
YOU'RE A DIVINER
PERHAPS
THEY WILL COME, MISS HENRIETT...

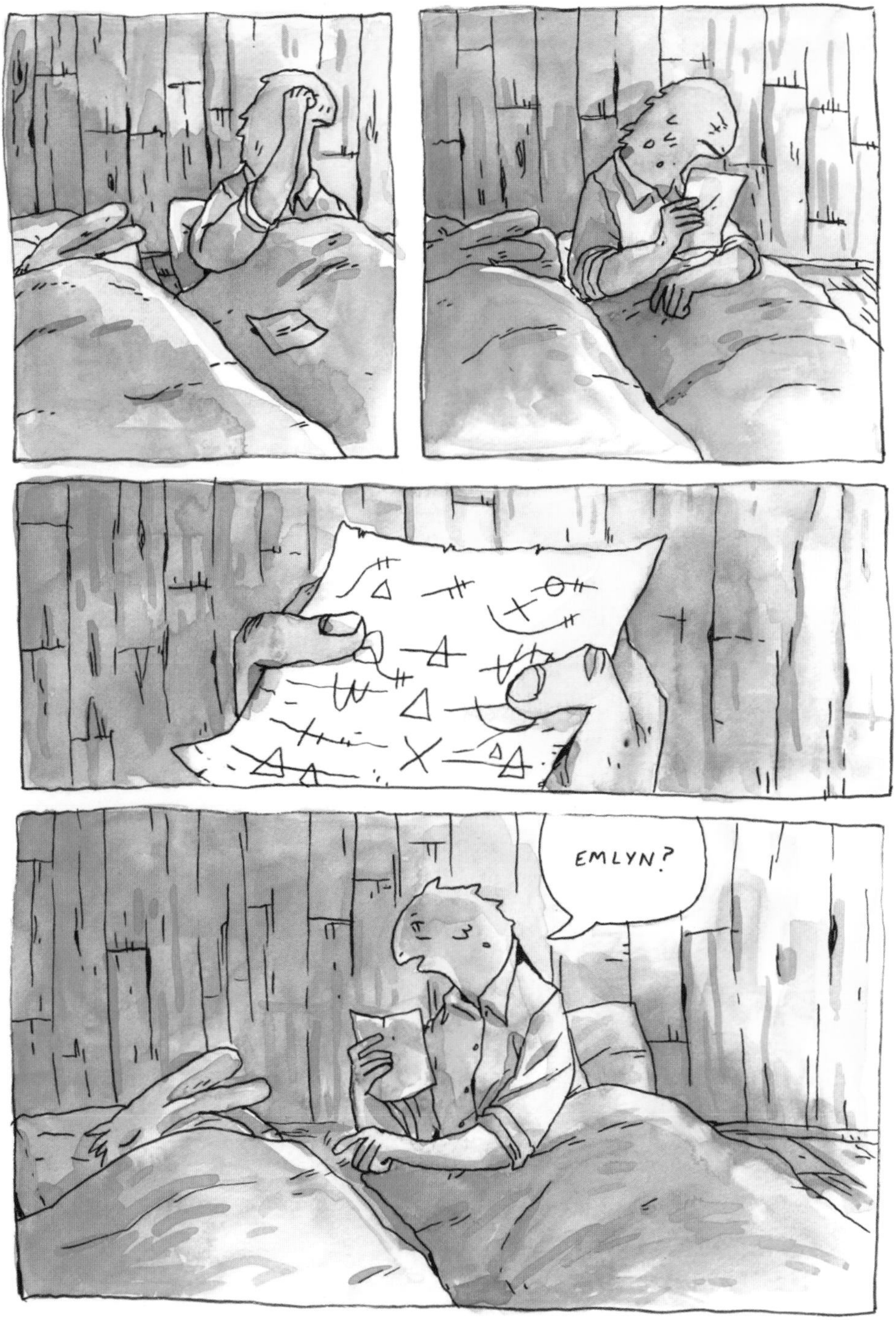
EMLYN?

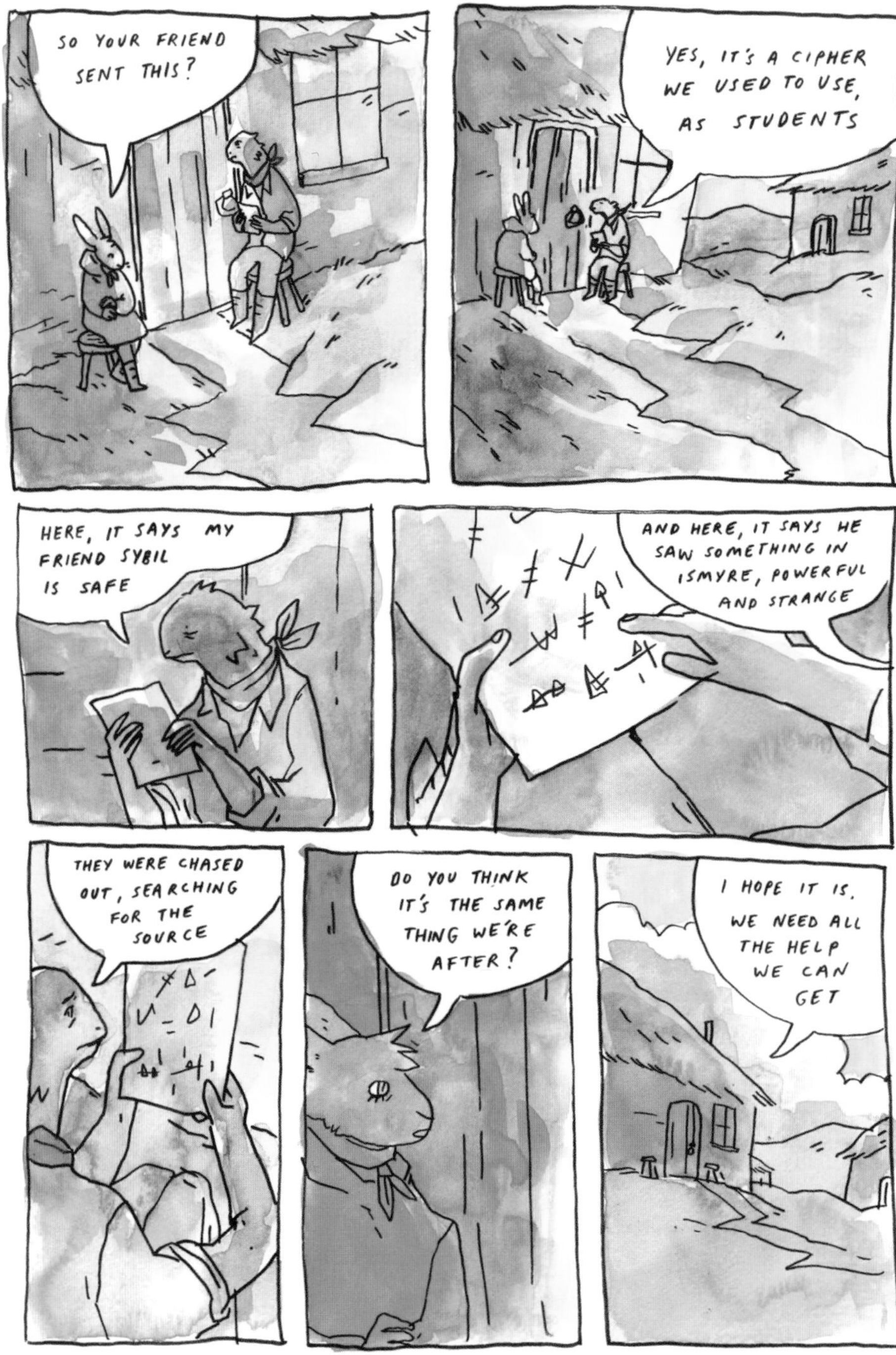
SO YOUR FRIEND SENT THIS?
YES, IT'S A CIPHER WE USED TO USE, AS STUDENTS
HERE, IT SAYS MY FRIEND SYBIL IS SAFE
AND HERE, IT SAYS HE SAW SOMETHING IN ISMYRE, POWERFUL AND STRANGE
THEY WERE CHASED OUT, SEARCHING FOR THE SOURCE
DO YOU THINK IT'S THE SAME THING WE'RE AFTER?
I HOPE IT IS. WE NEED ALL THE HELP WE CAN GET

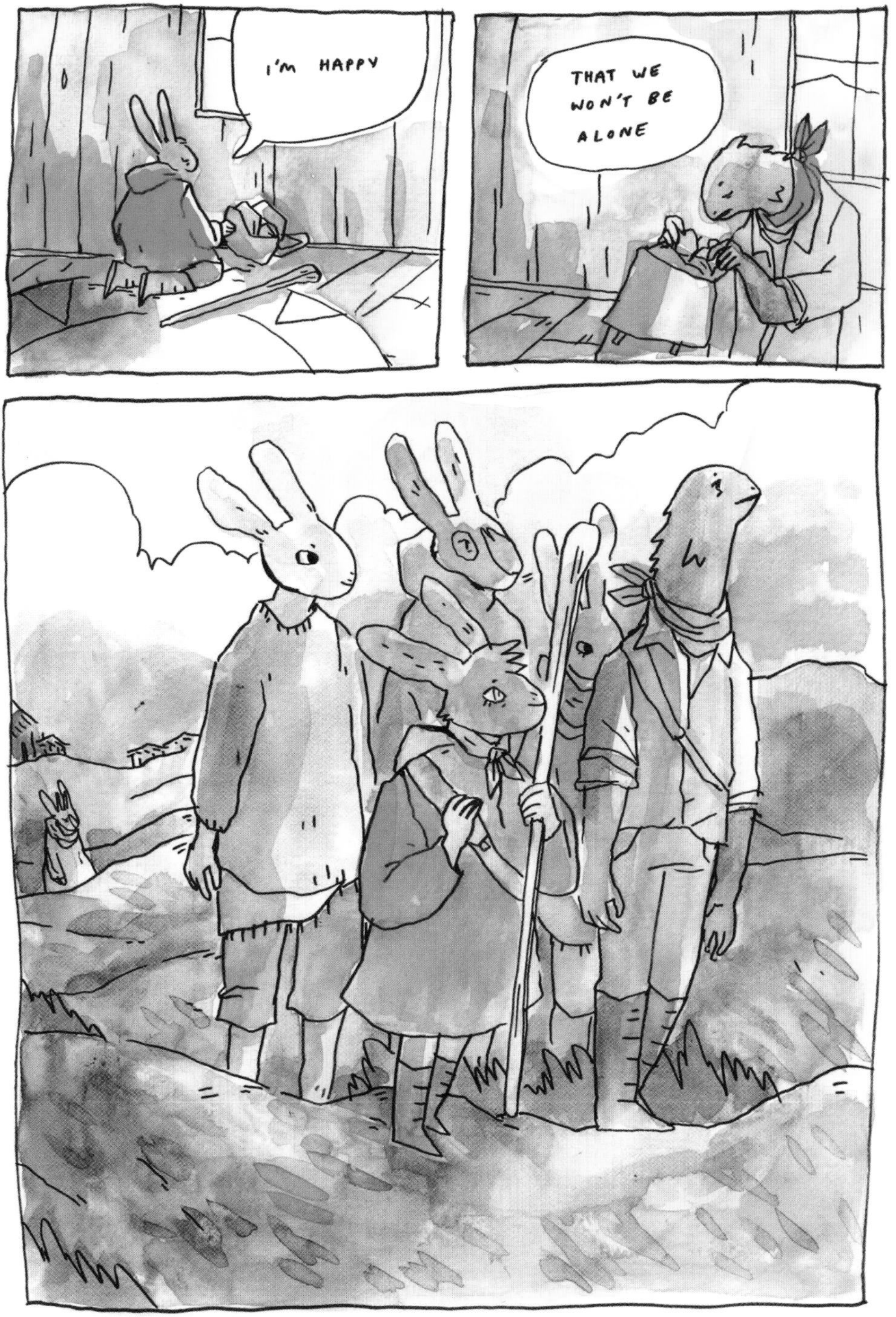
I'M HAPPY
THAT WE WON'T BE ALONE

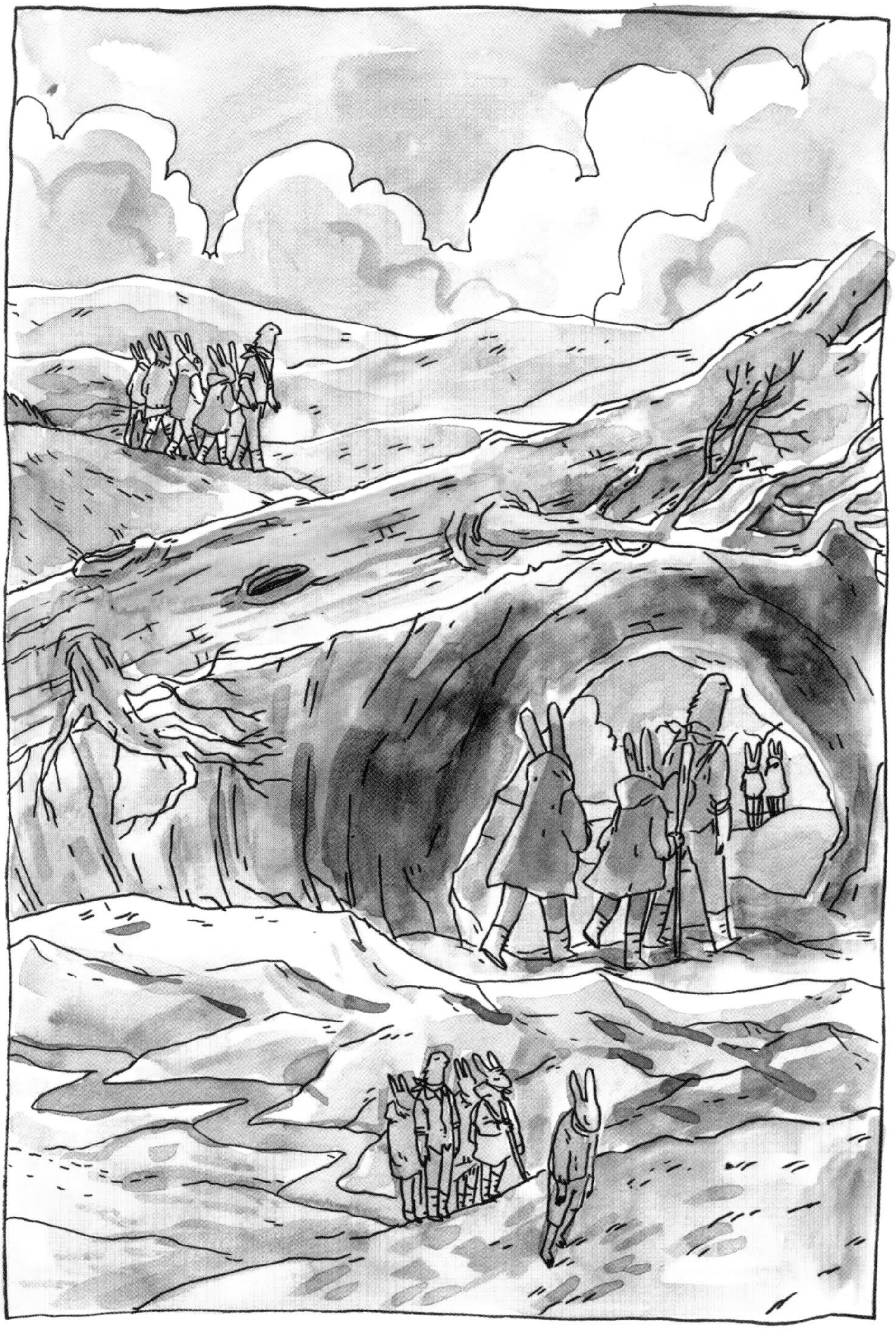

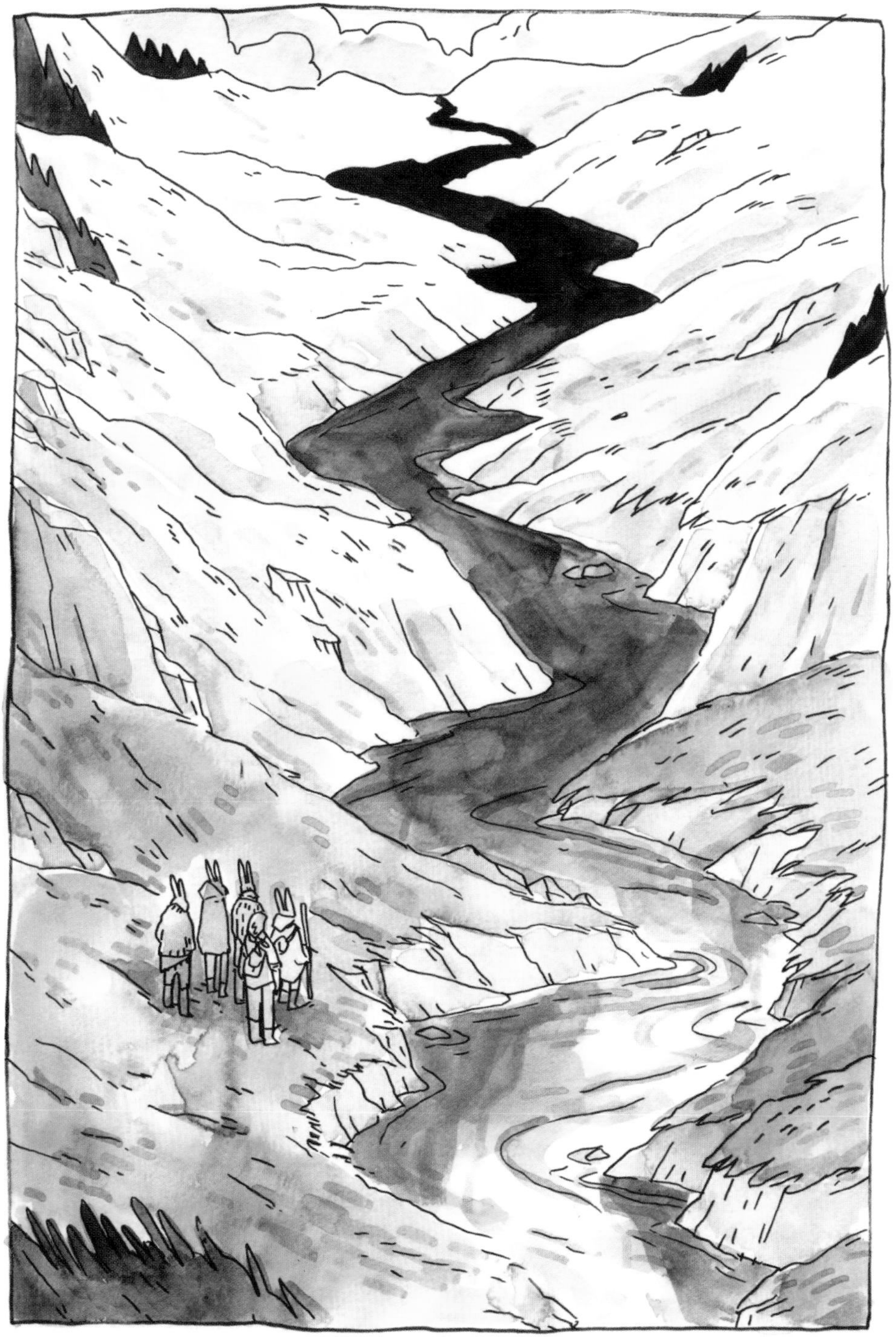

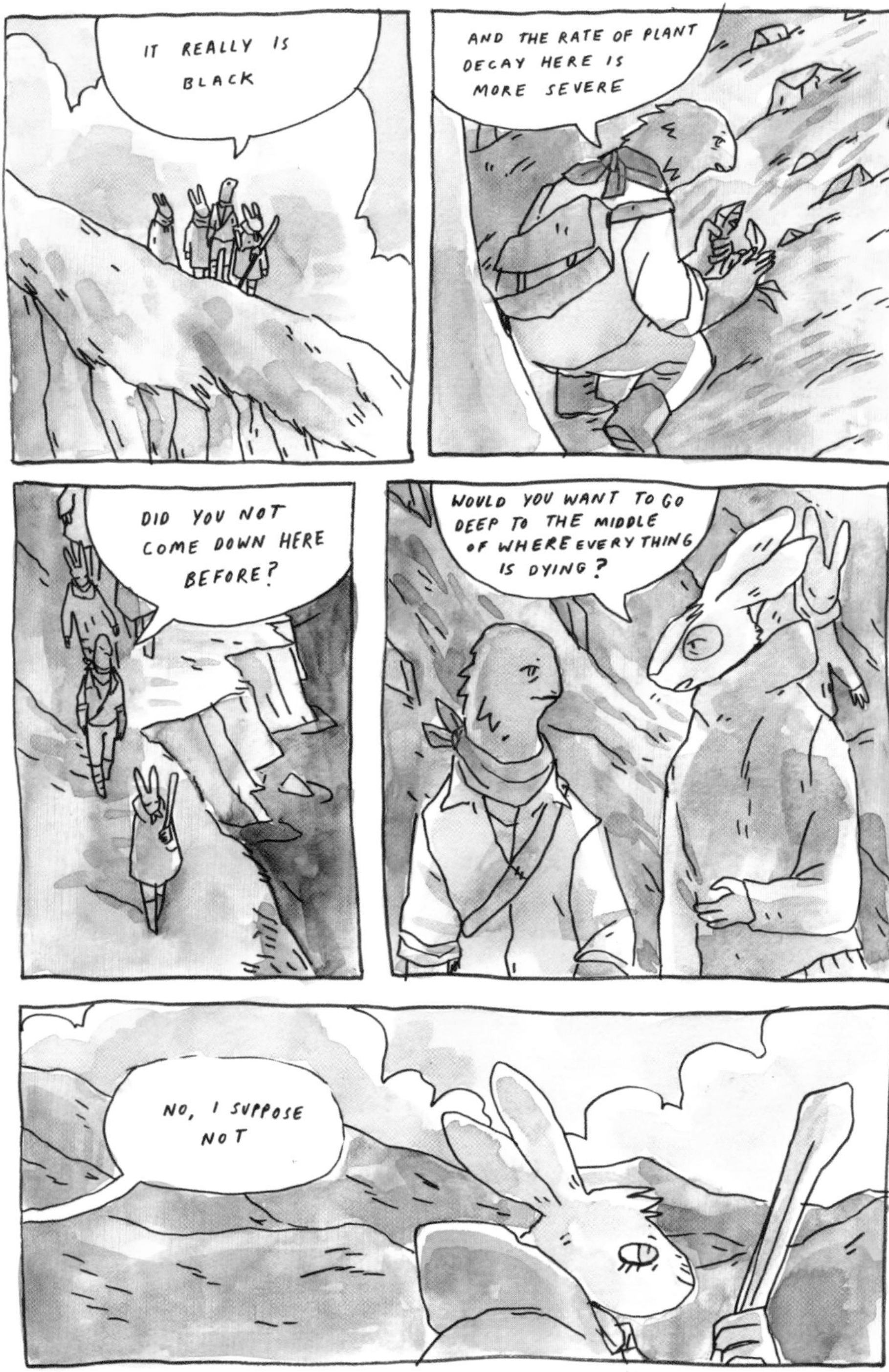
IT REALLY IS BLACK
AND THE RATE OF PLANT DECAY HERE IS MORE SEVERE
DID YOU NOT COME DOWN HERE BEFORE?
WOULD YOU WANT TO GO DEEP TO THE MIDDLE OF WHERE EVERYTHING IS DYING?
NO, I SUPPOSE NOT

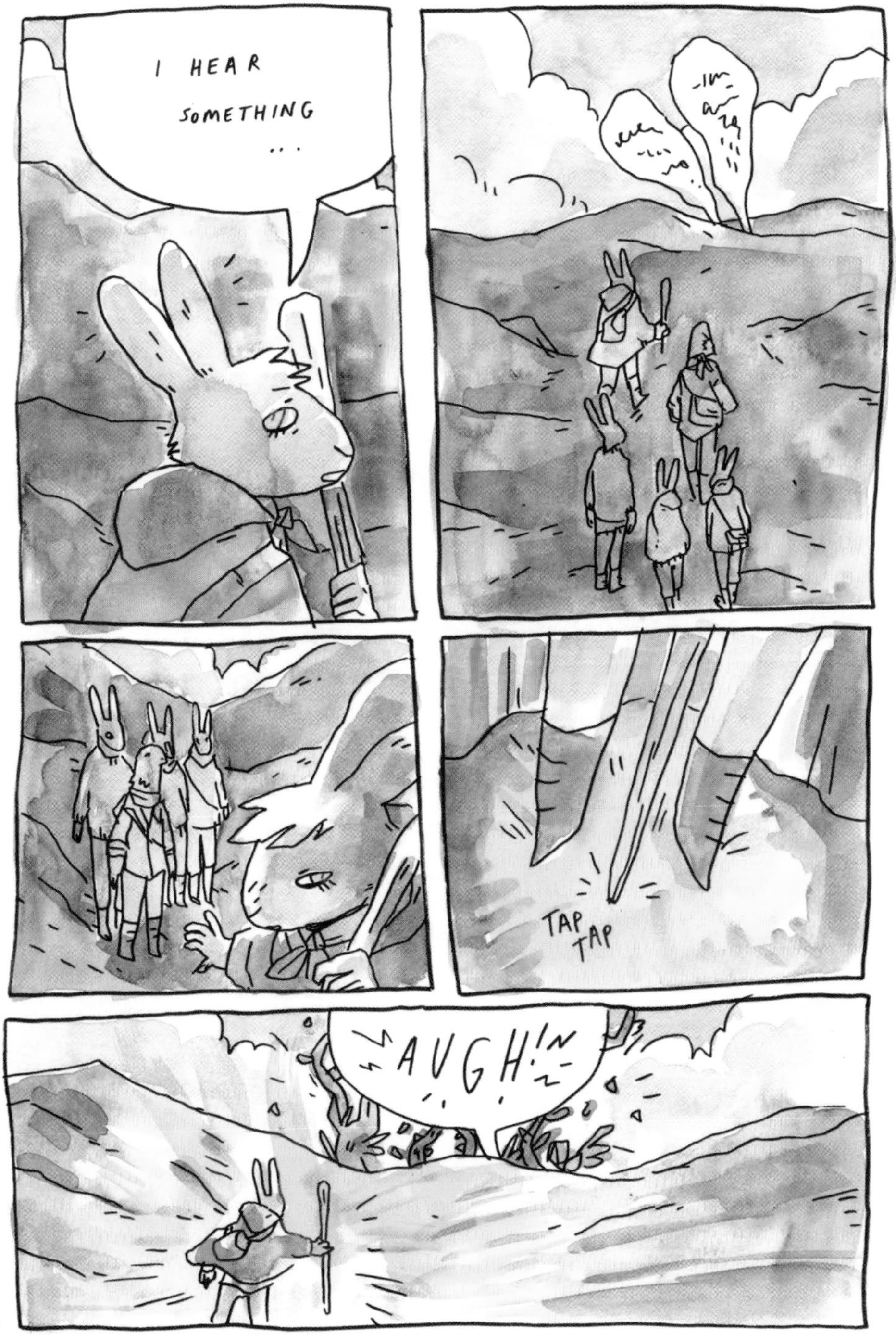
I HEAR SOMETHING ...
TAP TAP
AUGH!

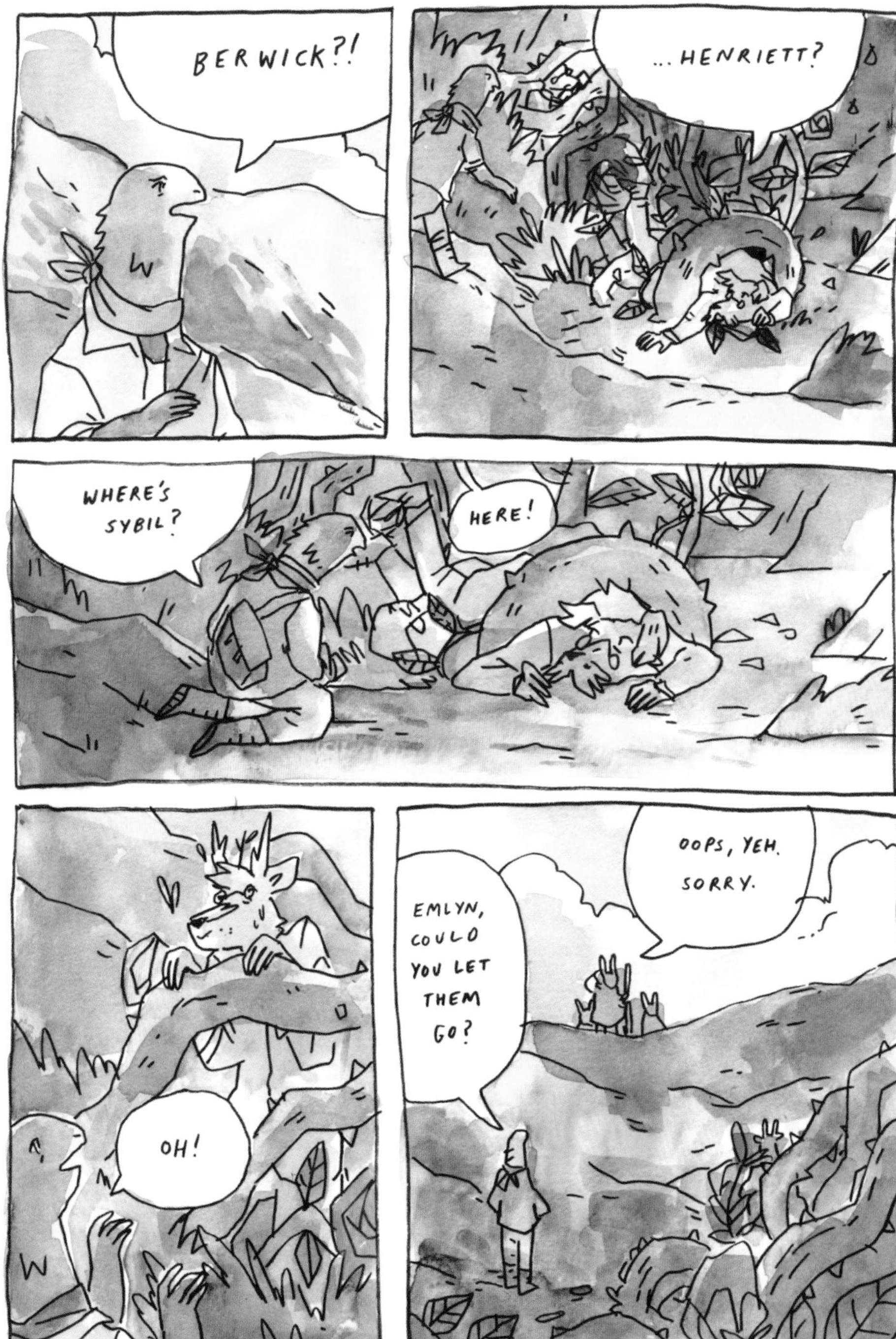
BERWICK?!
...HENRIETT?
WHERE'S SYBIL?
HERE!
OH!
OOPS, YEH. SORRY.
EMLYN, COULD YOU LET THEM GO?

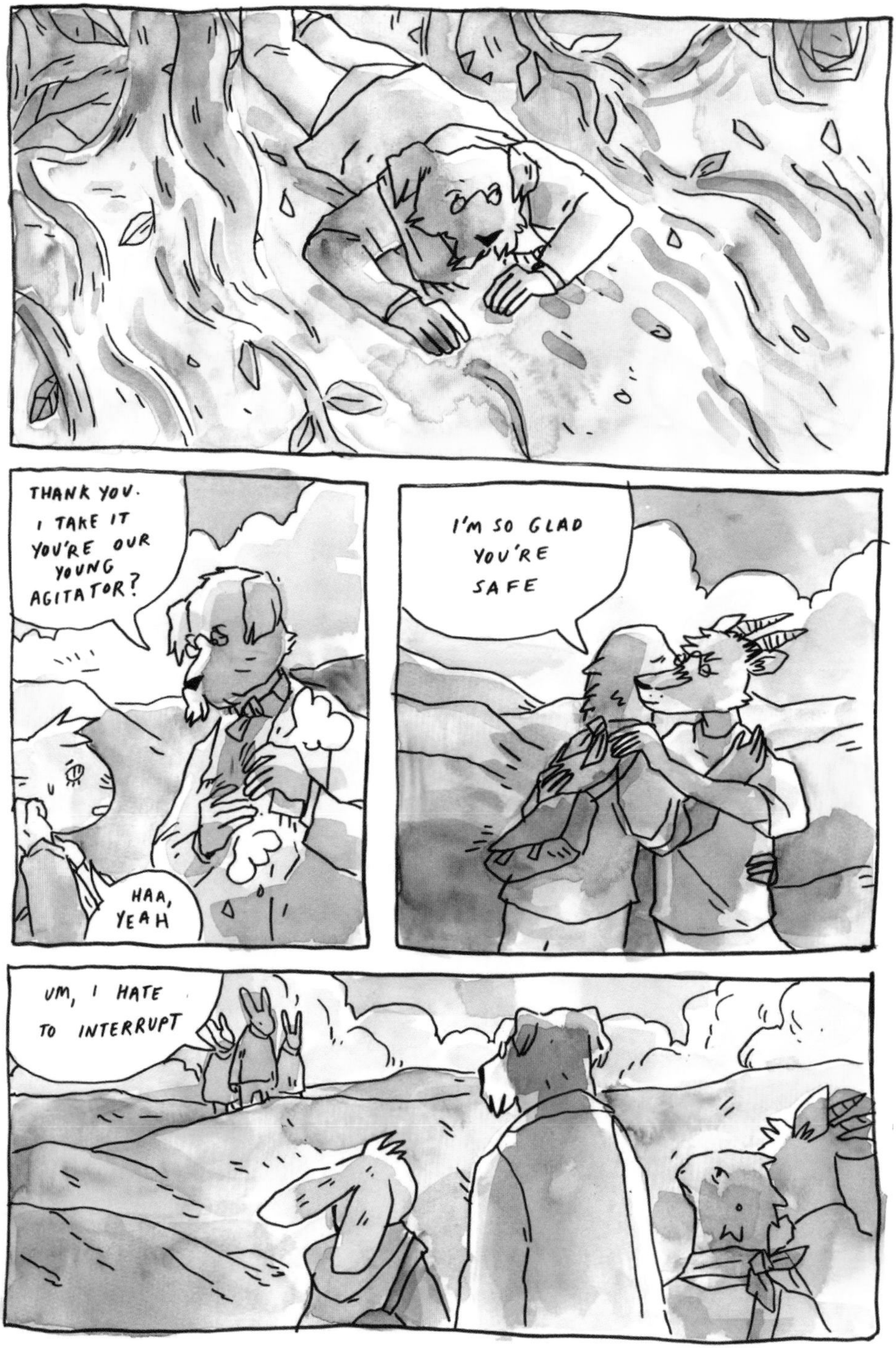
THANK YOU. I TAKE IT YOU'RE OUR YOUNG AGITATOR?
HAA, YEAH
I'M SO GLAD YOU'RE SAFE
UM, I HATE TO INTERRUPT

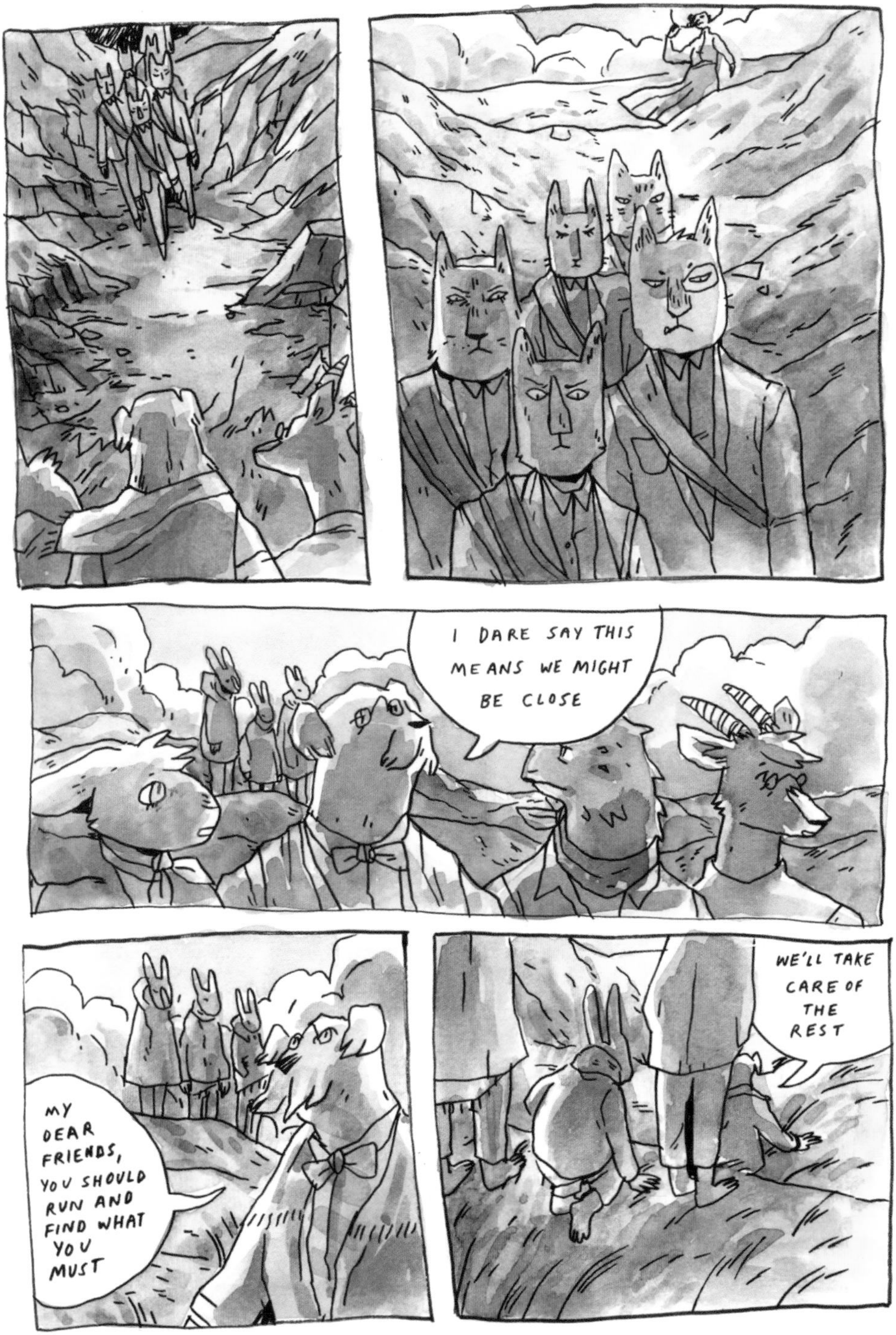

I DARE SAY THIS MEANS WE MIGHT BE CLOSE
MY DEAR FRIENDS, YOU SHOULD RUN AND FIND WHAT YOU MUST
WE'LL TAKE CARE OF THE REST

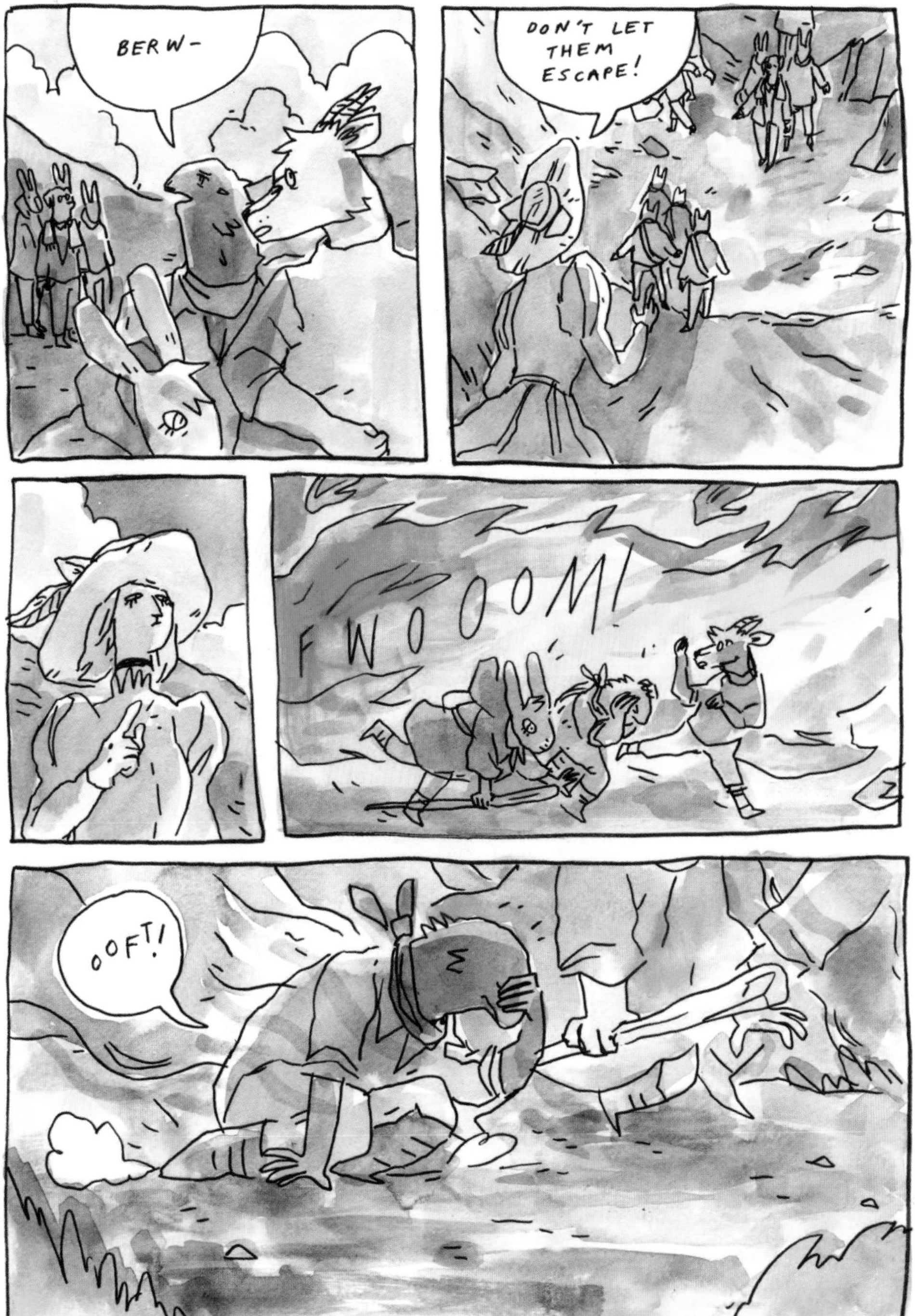
BERW-
DON'T LET THEM ESCAPE!
FWOOOM!
OOFT!

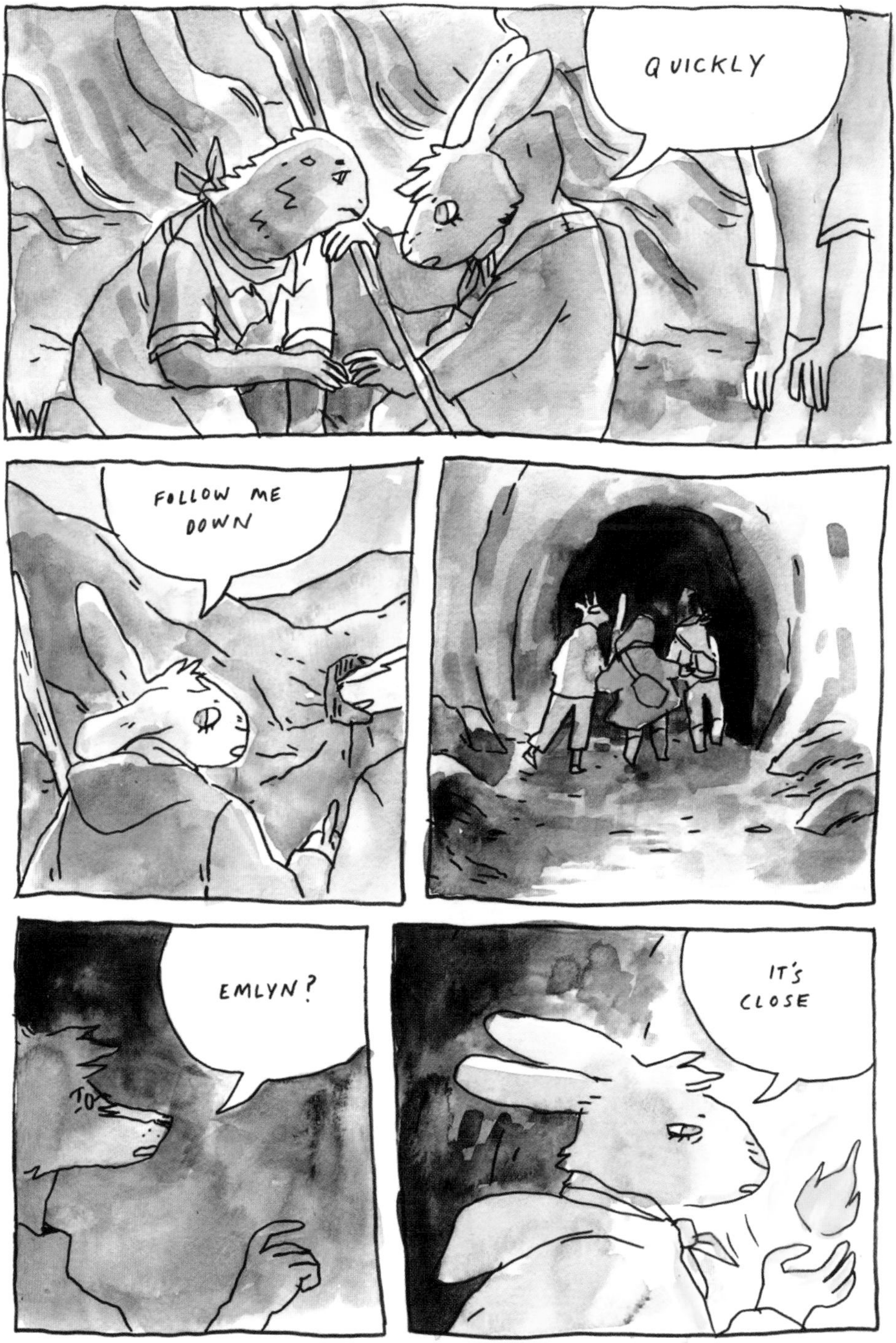
QUICKLY
FOLLOW ME DOWN
EMLYN?
IT'S CLOSE

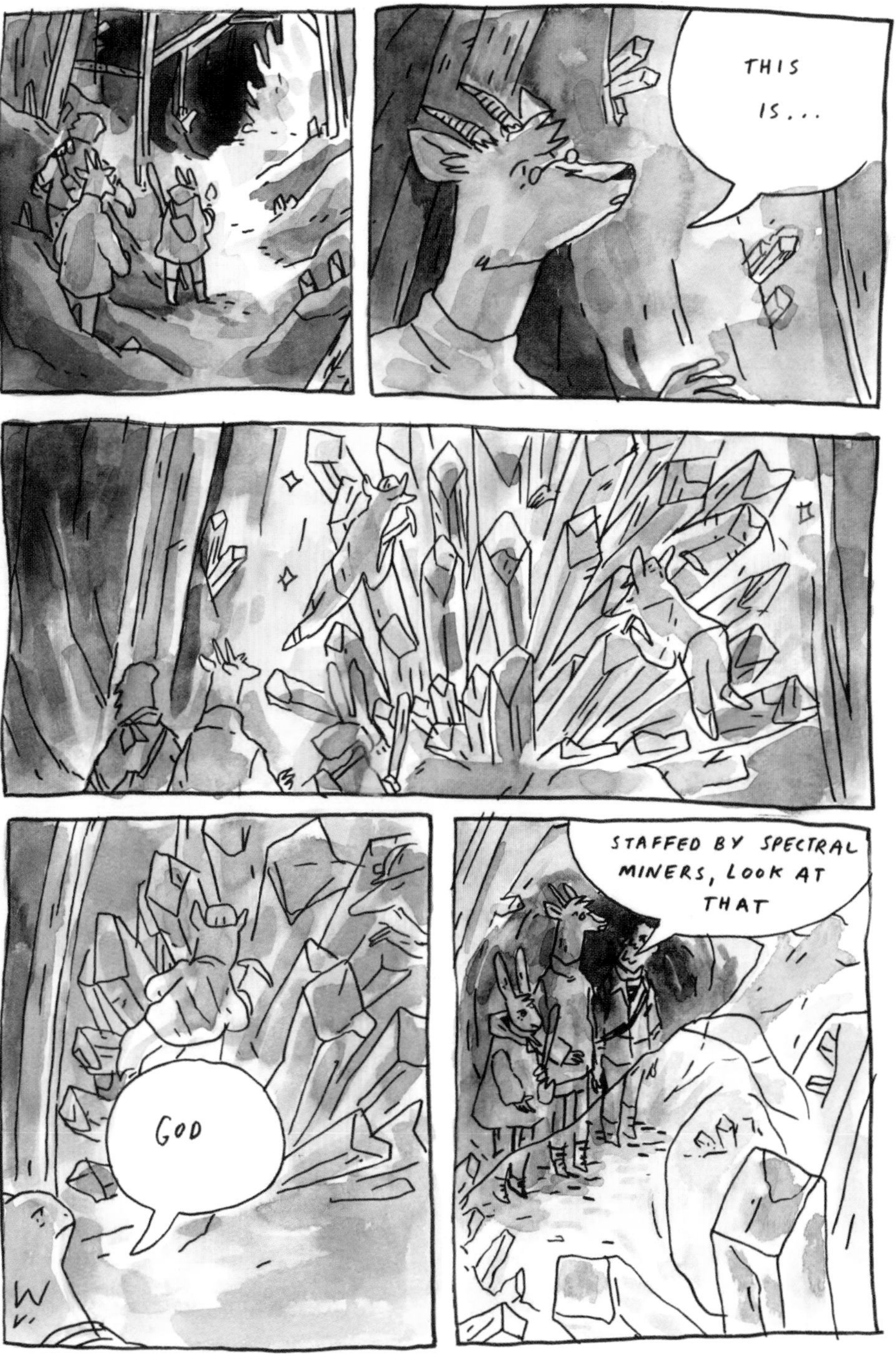
THIS IS...
GOD
STAFFED BY SPECTRAL MINERS, LOOK AT THAT

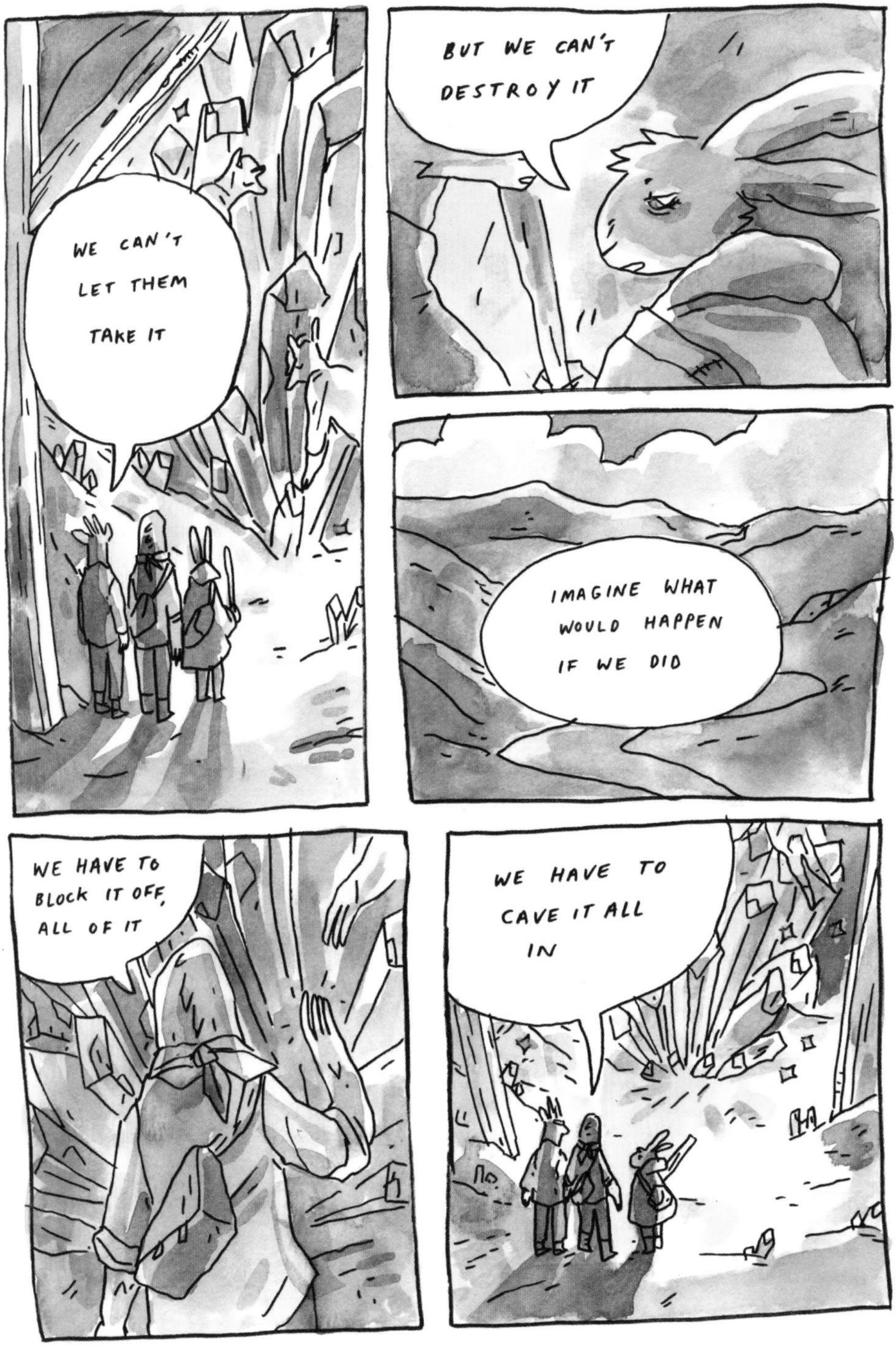
WE CAN'T LET THEM TAKE IT
BUT WE CAN'T DESTROY IT
IMAGINE WHAT WOULD HAPPEN IF WE DID
WE HAVE TO BLOCK IT OFF, ALL OF IT
WE HAVE TO CAVE IT ALL IN

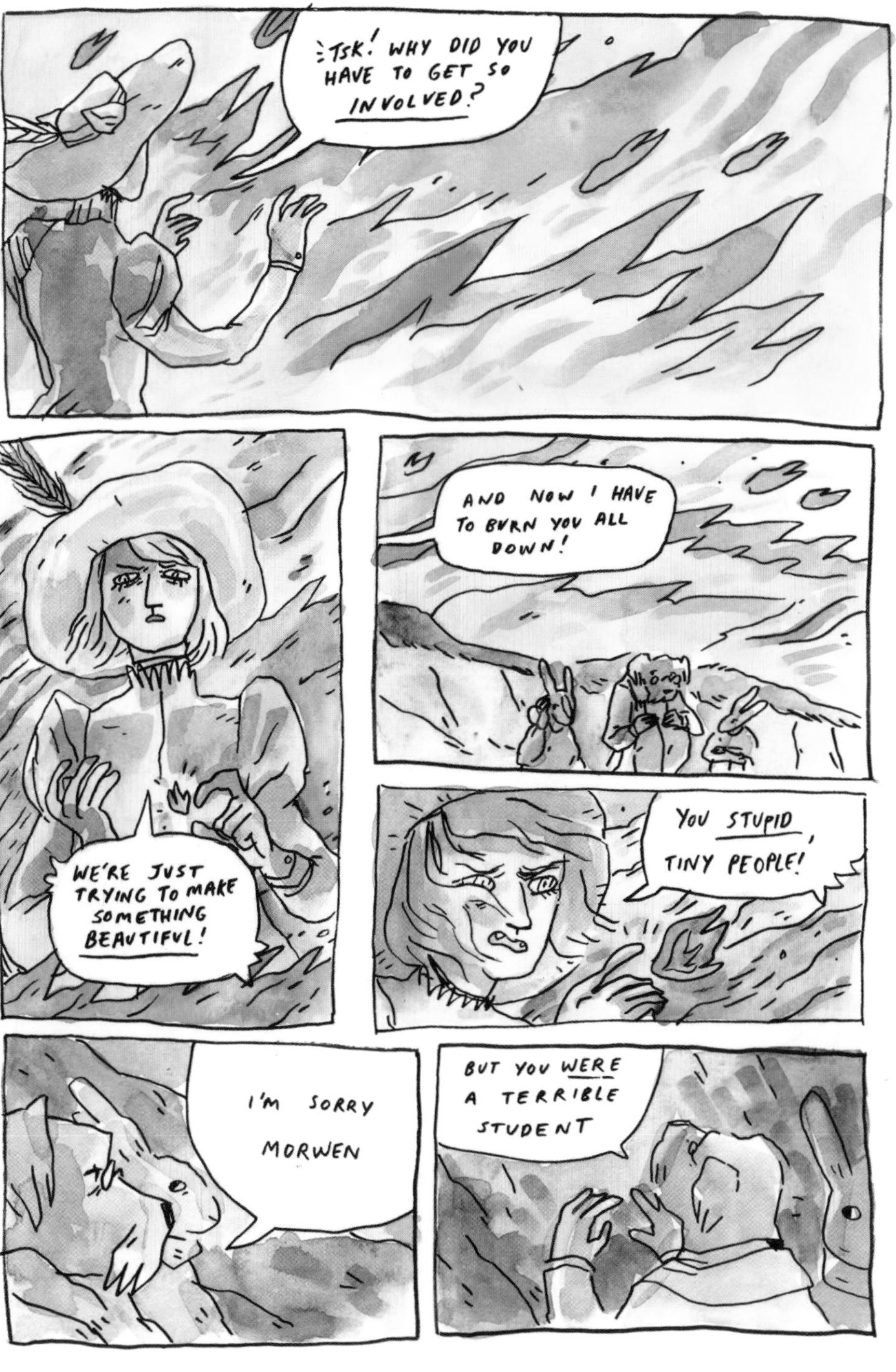
TSK! WHY DID YOU HAVE TO GET SO INVOLVED?
WE'RE JUST TRYING TO MAKE SOMETHING BEAUTIFUL!
AND NOW I HAVE TO BURN YOU ALL DOWN!
YOU STUPID, TINY PEOPLE!
I'M SORRY MORWEN
BUT YOU WERE A TERRIBLE STUDENT

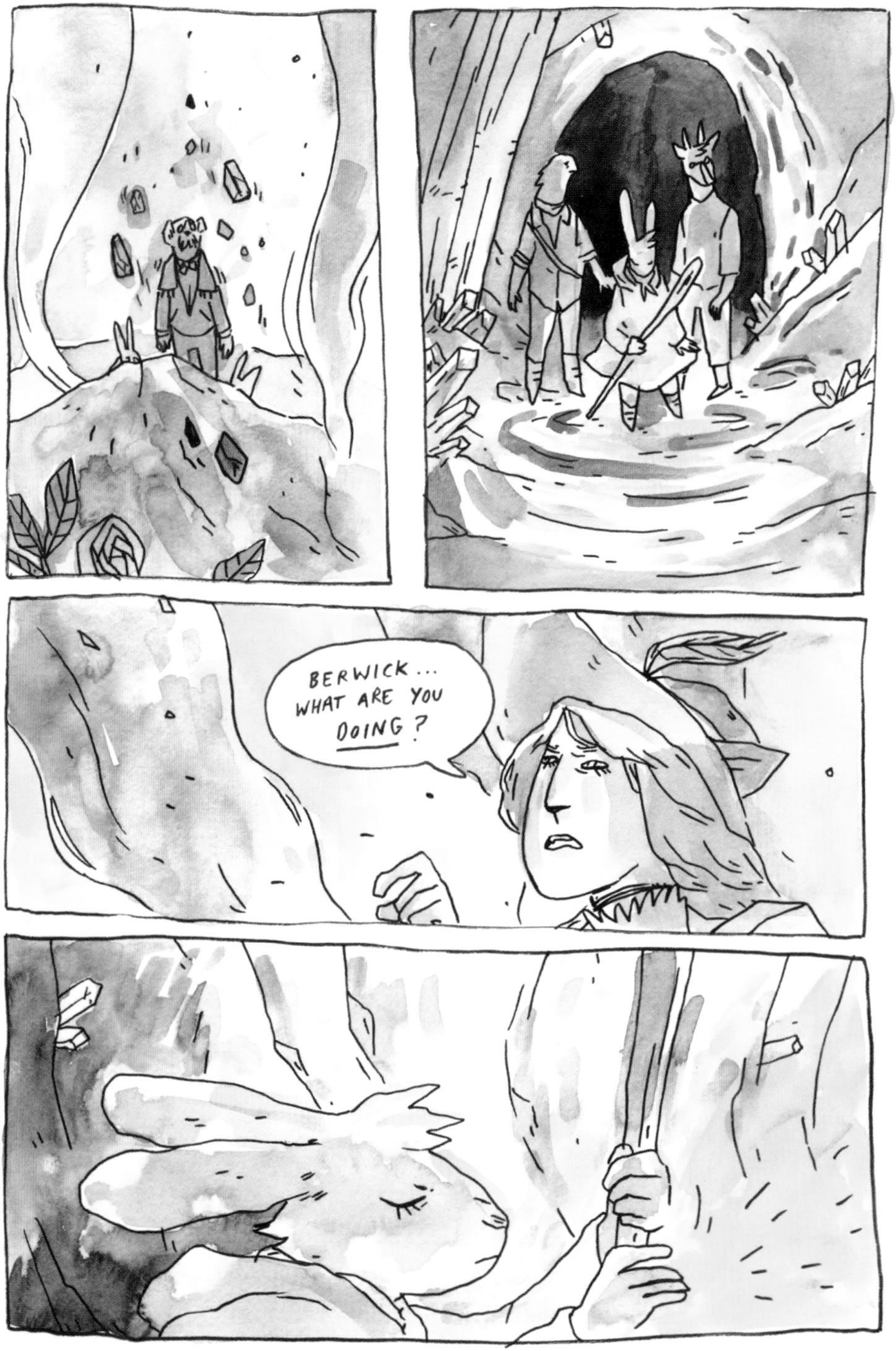
BERWICK... WHAT ARE YOU DOING?

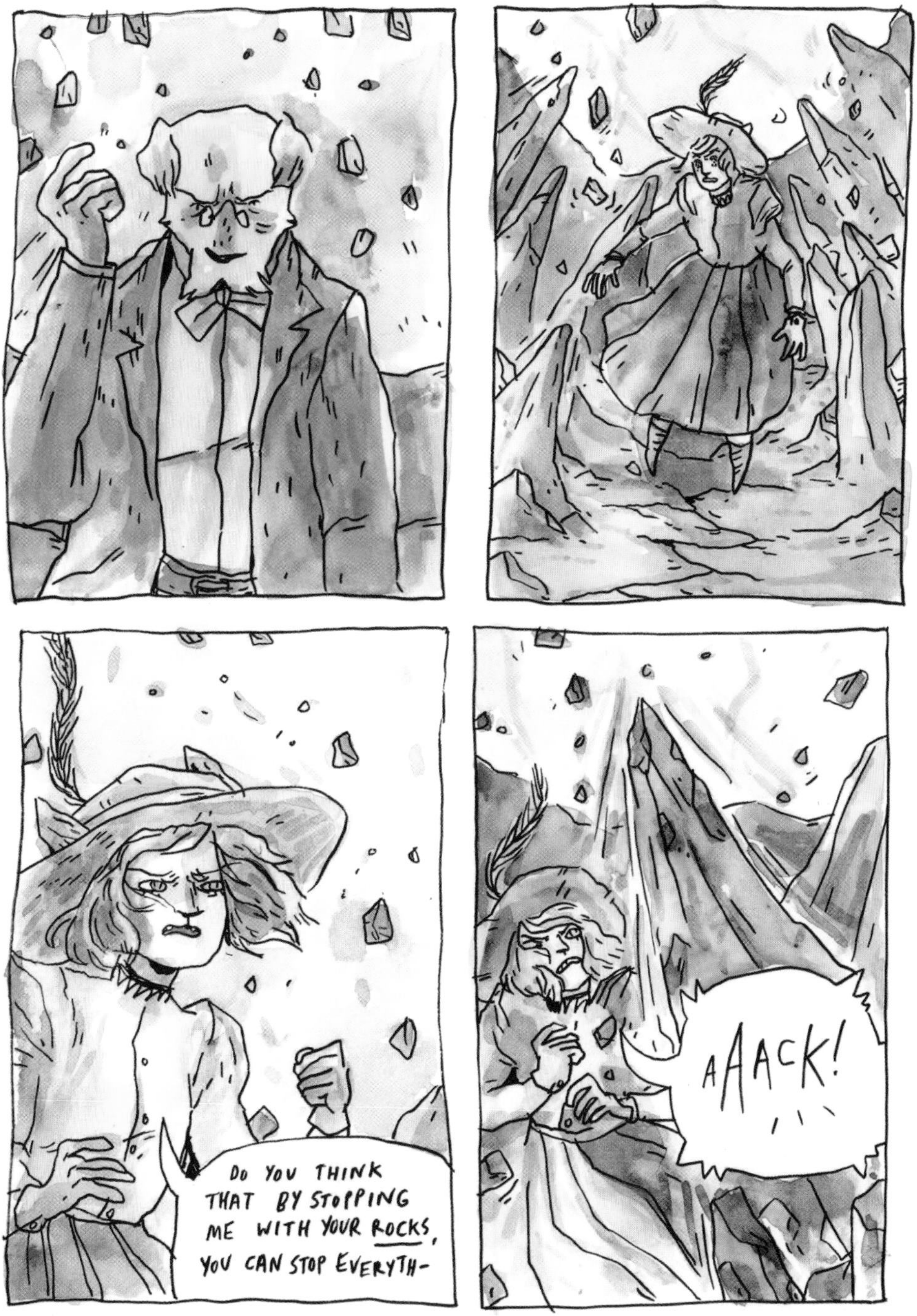
DO YOU THINK THAT BY STOPPING ME WITH YOUR ROCKS, YOU CAN STOP EVERYTH-
AAACK!

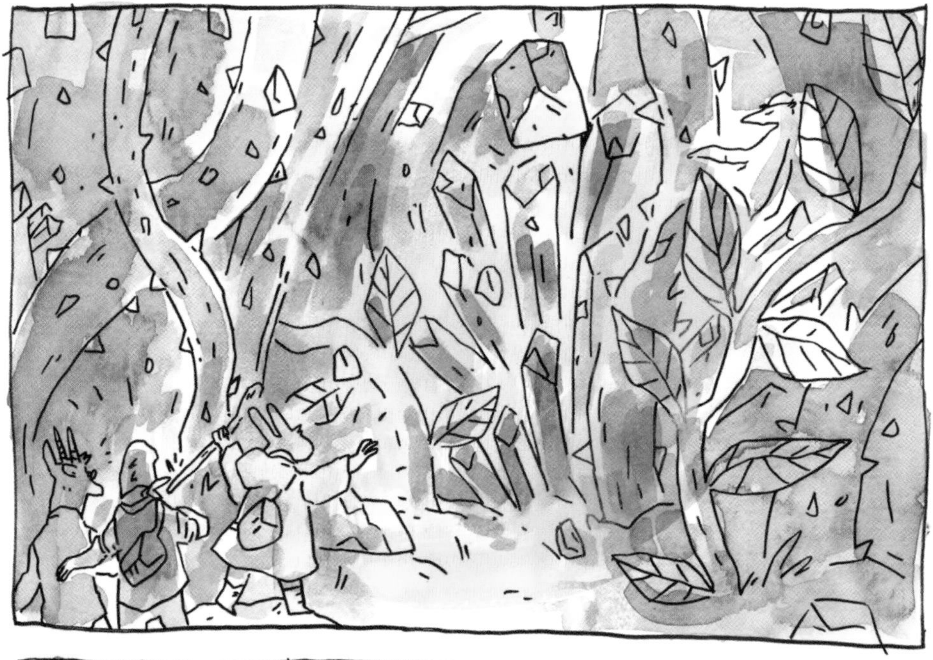

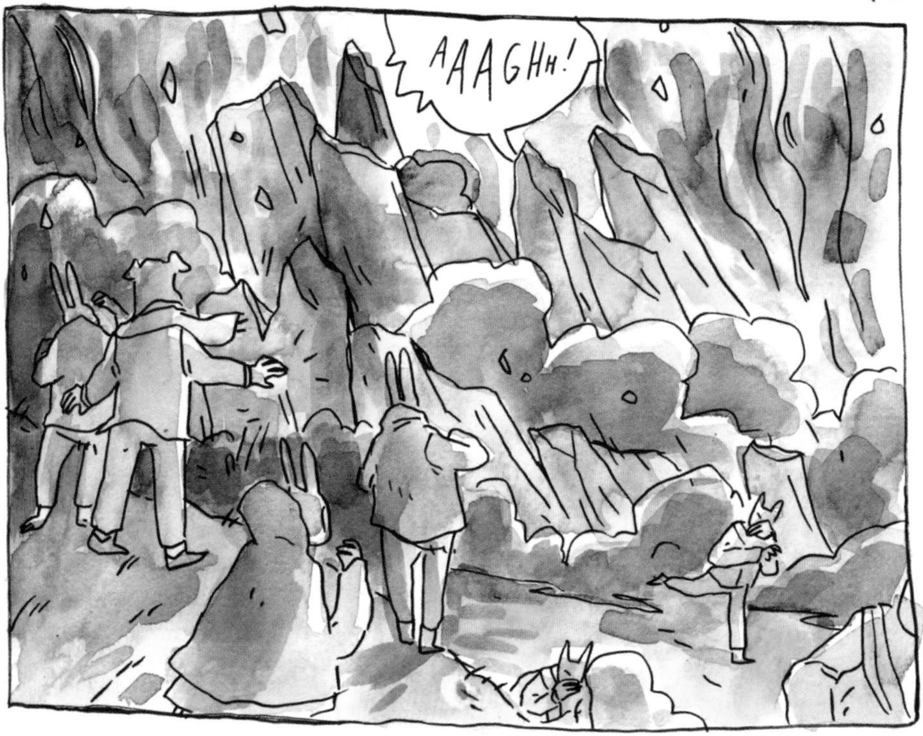
AAAGHH!

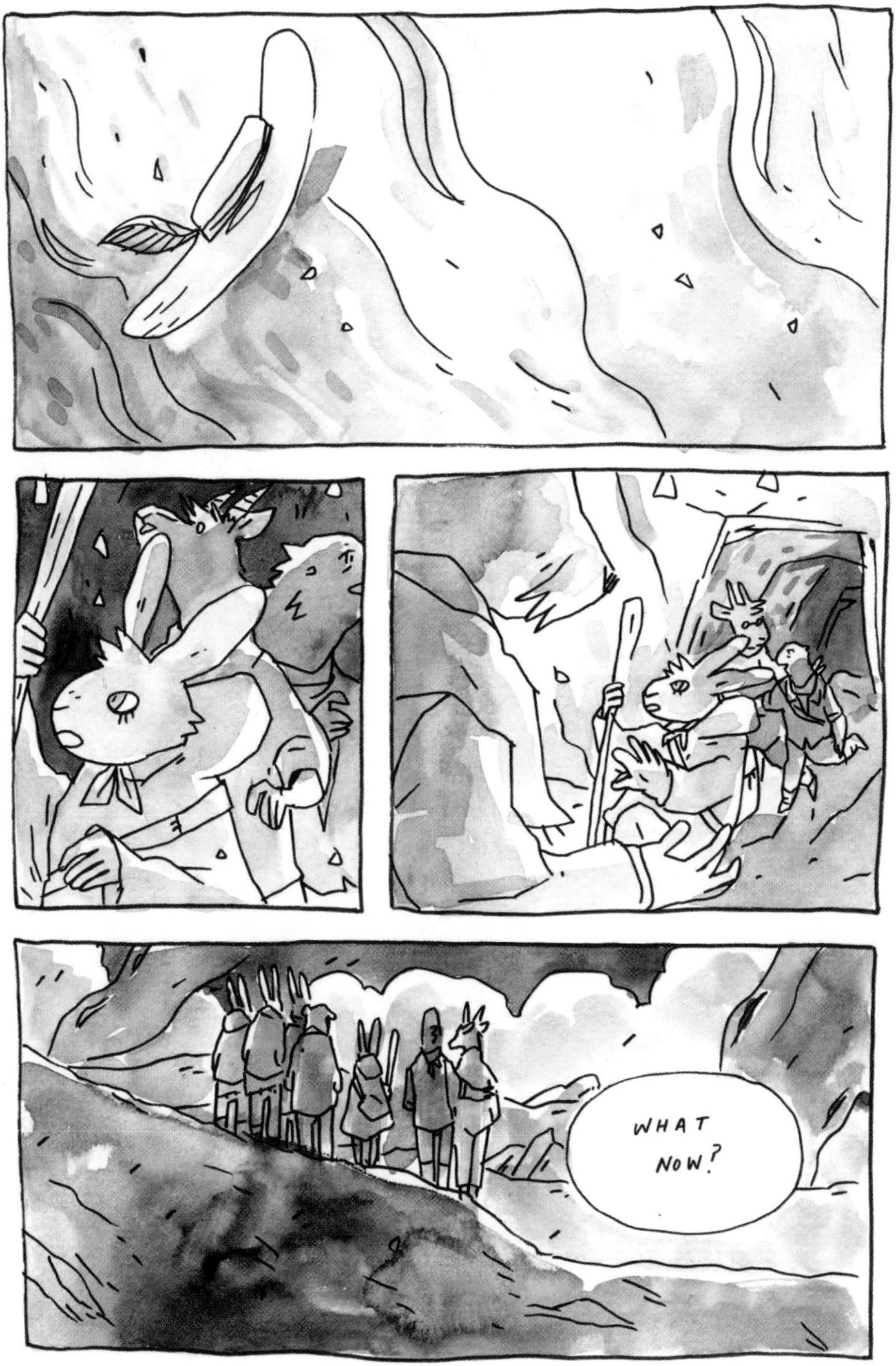
WHAT NOW?

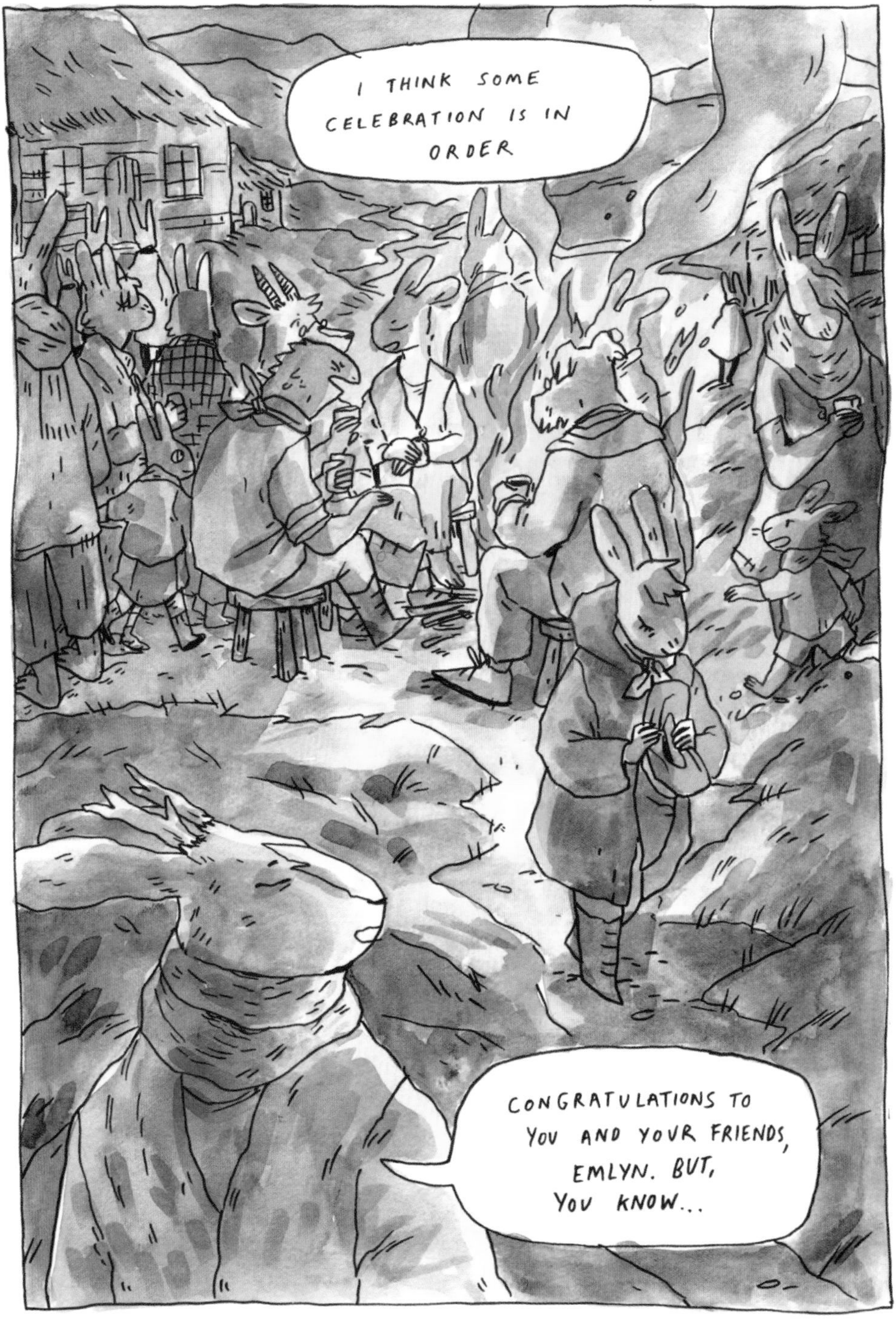
I THINK SOME CELEBRATION IS IN ORDER
CONGRATULATIONS TO YOU AND YOUR FRIENDS, EMLYN. BUT, YOU KNOW...

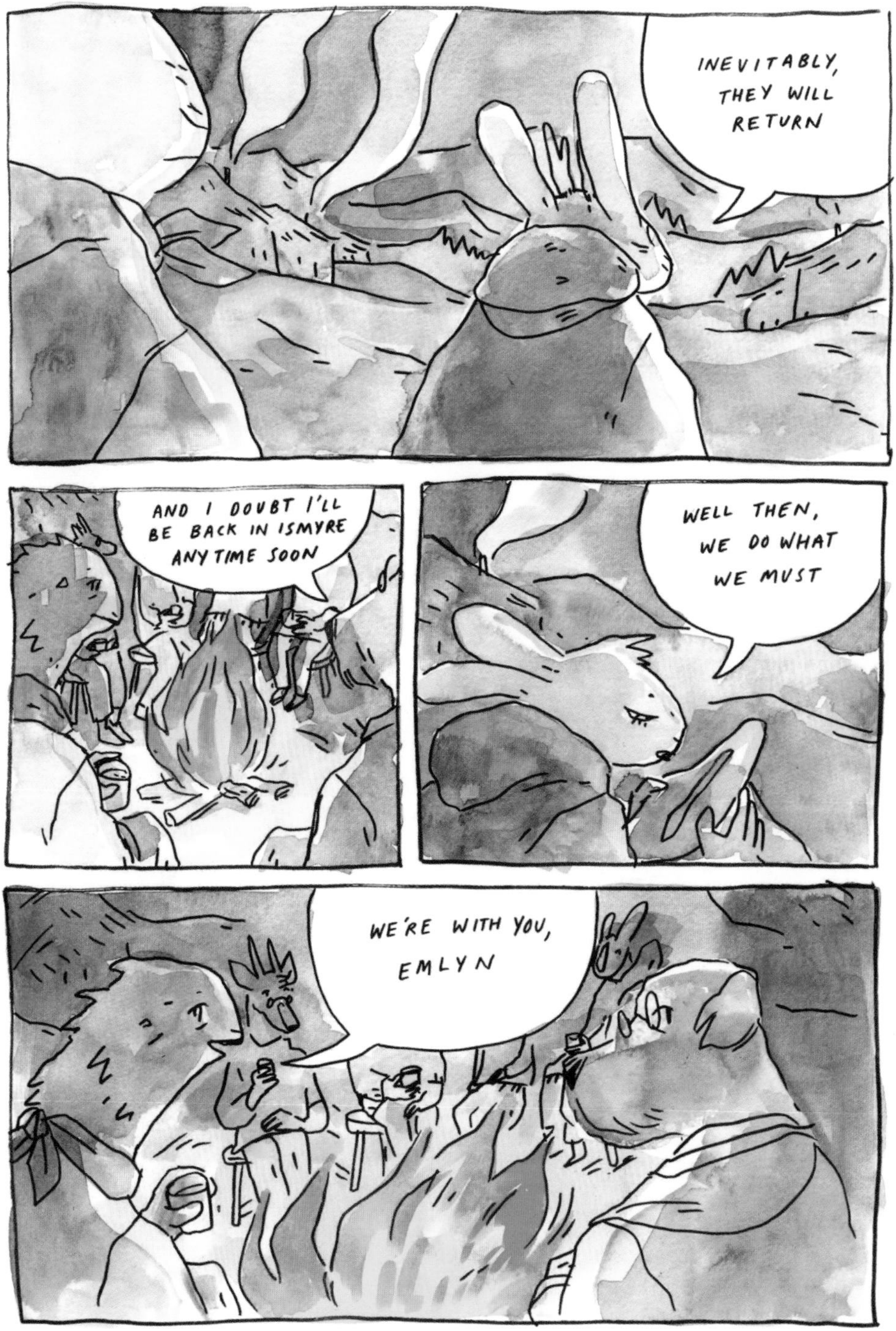
INEVITABLY, THEY WILL RETURN
AND I DOUBT I'LL BE BACK IN ISMYRE ANYTIME SOON
WELL THEN, WE DO WHAT WE MUST
WE'RE WITH YOU, EMLYN

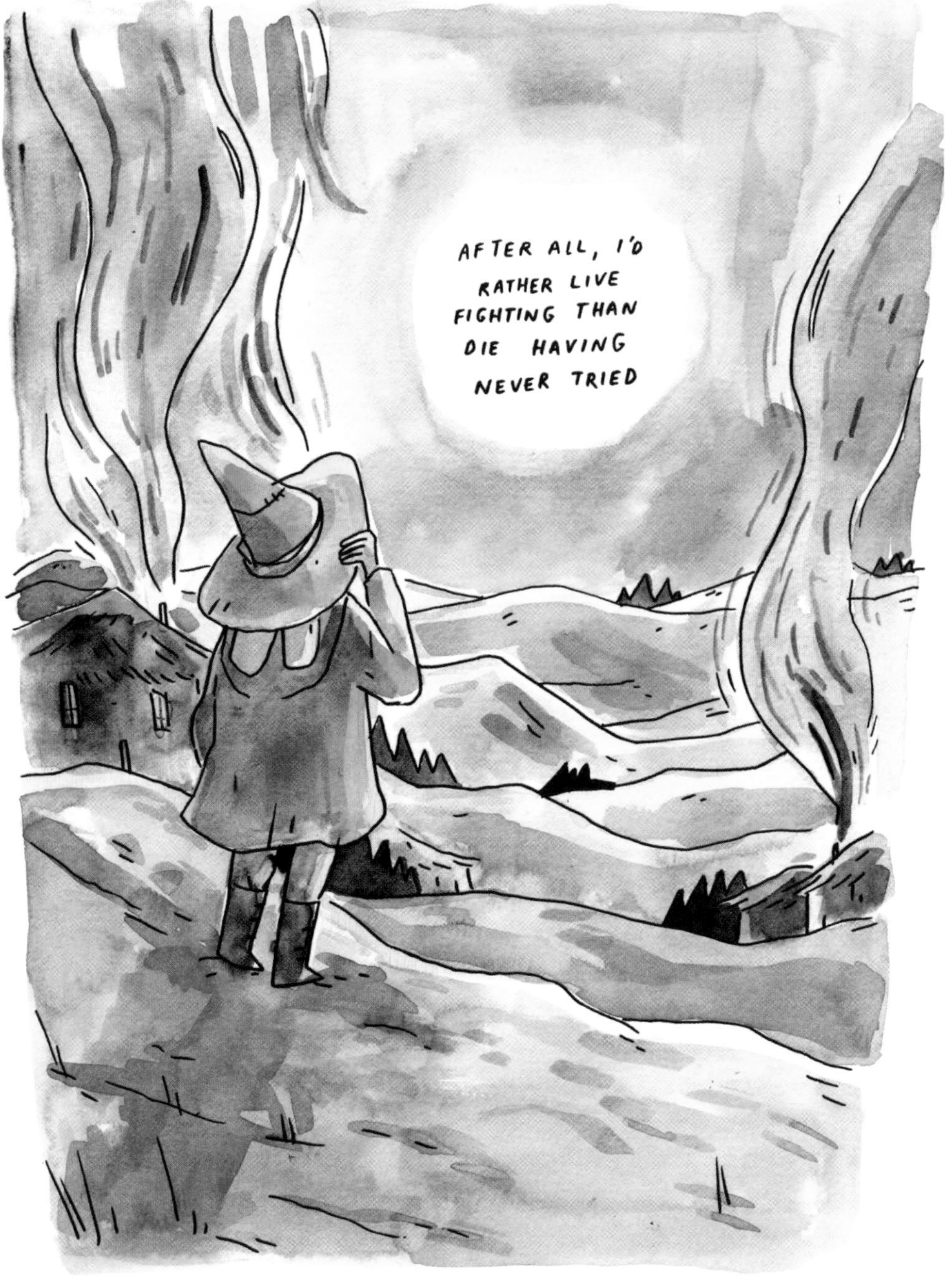
AFTER ALL, I'D RATHER LIVE FIGHTING THAN DIE HAVING NEVER TRIED

THANKS TO EVERYONE FOR
YOUR SUPPORT! ESPECIALLY
CHRIS NEAL, WHO DREW THE MAP
AND ANNA CAMPBELL, WHO
WE MISS EVERY DAY AND
INSPIRES FOREVER

FIGHT THE GOOD FIGHT

Published by Avery Hill Publishing, 2018

10 9 8 7 6 5 4 3 2 1

First published in the UK in 2018 by
Avery Hill Publishing
Unit 8
5 Durham Yard
London
EC2 6QF

A CIP record for this book is available from the British Library

ISBN: 978 1 910395 43 1

B. Mure
www.bmurecreative.co.uk

Avery Hill Publishing
www.averyhillpublishing.com